Modern Critical Interpretations

Genesis

Modern Critical Interpretations

These and other titles in preparation

Genesis

Edited and with an introduction by

Harold Bloom
Sterling Professor of the Humanities
Yale University

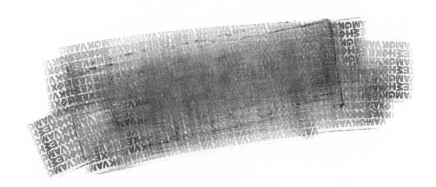

Chelsea House Publishers ◊ 1986
NEW YORK ◊ NEW HAVEN ◊ PHILADELPHIA

11540

222
Blo

©1986 by Chelsea House Publishers, a division of
Chelsea House Educational Communications, Inc.
133 Christopher Street, New York, NY 10014
345 Whitney Avenue, New Haven, CT 06511
5014 West Chester Pike, Edgemont, PA 19028

Introduction © 1986 by Harold Bloom

Printed and bound in the United States of America

∞ The paper used in this publication meets the minimum requirements of
the American National Standard for Permanence of Paper for Printed Library
Materials, Z39.48-1984.

Library of Congress Cataloging-in-Publication Data
Genesis.
    (Modern critical interpretations)
    Bibliography: p.
    Includes index.
    1. Bible. O.T. Genesis—Criticism, interpretation,
etc. I. Bloom, Harold. II. Series.
BS1235.2.G38 1986   222'.1106   86-9748
ISBN 0-87754-910-9

Contents

Editor's Note

This book brings together essays in literary criticism upon Genesis, though I have interpreted "literary criticism" in the widest possible sense, because the Bible demands no less. The essays are arranged here in the chronological sequence of their original publication. I am grateful to Hillary Kelleher for her devoted care in helping to research and edit this volume.

The editor's introduction follows the scholarly influence of the late Ephraim Speiser by arguing for the separate authorial presence of the Yahwist or "J writer," judged here to be the strongest and most original of all ancient Hebrew writers. Erich Auerbach's account of the Akedah, or attempted sacrifice of Isaac, acutely analyzes the singular representation of reality that is wholly characteristic of the Bible.

What Kenneth Burke calls his "logology" is applied by him, with grand high-spiritedness, to aspects of the first three chapters of Genesis. A very different vision is manifested by the eminent scholar of political philosophy Leo Strauss, in his contrast of Hebrew and Greek ideas of origin. Altogether less normative than Strauss, Martin Buber gives an interpretation of the Tree of Knowledge that is consonant with his idealizing mythology of dialogue.

Robert Alter, a pioneer in reading biblical narrative by literary means, tries to suggest the "composite artistry" by which the redactors were able to fuse the all-but-contradictory visions of the J writer and the Priestly author.

Two opposing readings of Wrestling Jacob follow, starting with the celebrated textual analysis by Roland Barthes, and continuing with my own rather antithetical interpretation. James S. Ackerman's exegesis of the Joseph saga illuminates not only the exemplary figure of Joseph but the more problematic Judah as well. Finally, Meir Sternberg's intricate structural investigation of the wooing of Rebekah reveals the complex perspectival relations that are so crucial to the narrative patternings of Genesis.

Introduction

To my best knowledge, it was the Harvard historian of religion George Foot Moore who first called the religion of the rabbis of the second century of the Common Era "normative Judaism." Let me simplify by centering on one of those rabbis, surely the grandest: normative Judaism is the religion of Akiba. That vigorous scholar, patriot, and martyr may be regarded as the standard by which any other Jewish religious figure must be judged. If your faith and praxis share enough with Akiba's, then you too are a representative of normative Judaism. If not, then probably not. There is a charming legend in which Moses attends Akiba's seminar, and goes away baffled by the sage's interpretation—of Moses! But the deepest implication of the legend, as I read it, is that Akiba's strong misreading of Moses was in no way weakened by the Mosaic bafflement.

The Great Original of the literary and oral traditions that merged into normative Judaism was the writer scholarly convention rather wonderfully chose to call "J." Since Kafka is the most legitimate descendant of one aspect of the antithetical J (Tolstoy and the early, pre-Coleridgean Wordsworth are the most authentic descendants of J's other side), I find it useful to adopt the formula "from J to K," in order to describe the uncanny or antithetical elements in J's narratives. The J who could have written *Hadji Murad* or *The Tale of Margaret* was the inevitable fountainhead of what eventually became normative Judaism. But this first, strongest, and still somehow most Jewish of all our writers also could have written "The Hunter Gracchus" or even "Josephine the Singer and the Mouse Folk." Indeed he wrote uncannier stories than Kafka lived to write. How those stories ever could have been acceptable or even comprehensible to the P authors or the Deuteronomist, to the Academy of Ezra or the Pharisees, let alone to Akiba and his colleagues, is a mystery that I have been trying to clarify by developing a critical concept of what I call "facticity," a kind of brute contingency by which an author's strength blinds and incarcerates a tradition of belated readership. But here I primarily want to describe the uncanniness of J's work, so as to break out of facticity, insofar as I am able to do so.

1

By "the uncanny" I mean Freud's concept, since that appears to be the authentic modern version of what once was called the Sublime. Freud defines "the uncanny" as being "in reality nothing new or foreign, but something familiar and old-established in the mind that has been estranged only by the process of repression." Since I myself, as a critic, am obsessed with the Sublime or Freud's "uncanny," I realize that my reading of any Sublime work or fragment is always dependent upon an estrangement, in which the repressed returns upon me to end that estrangement, but only momentarily. The uncanniness of the Yahwist exceeds that of all other writers, because in him both the estrangement and the return achieve maximum force.

Of course J himself is considered to be a fiction, variously referred to by scholars as a school, a tradition, a document, and a hypothesis. Well, Homer is perhaps a fiction too, and these days the slaves of critical fashion do not weary of proclaiming the death of the author, or at least the reduction of every author to the status of a Nietzschean fiction. But J is pragmatically the author-of-authors, in that his authority and originality constitute a difference that has made a difference. The teller of the tales of Jacob and of Joseph, of Moses and the Exodus, is a writer more inescapable than Shakespeare and more pervasive in our consciousness than Freud. J's only cultural rival would be an unlikely compound of Homer and Plato. Plato's contest with Homer seems to me to mark one of the largest differences between the ancient Greeks and the Hebrews. The agon for the mind of Athens found no equivalent in Jerusalem, and so the Yahwist still remains the mind of Jerusalem, everywhere that Jerusalem happens to be.

I do not believe that J was a fiction, and indeed J troubles me because his uncanniness calls into question my own conviction that every writer is belated, and so is always an inter-poet. J's freedom from belatedness rivals Shakespeare's, which is to say that J's originality is as intense as Shakespeare's. But J wrote twenty-five hundred years before Shakespeare, and that timespan bewilders comparison. I am going to sketch J's possible circumstances and purposes, in order to hazard a description of J's tone, or of the uncanniness of his stance as a writer. Not much in my sketch will flout received scholarship, but necessarily I will have to go beyond the present state of biblical scholarship, since it cannot even decide precisely which texts are J's, or even revised by others from J. My attempt at transcending scholarship is simply a literary critic's final reliance upon her or his own sense of a text, or what I have called the necessity of misreading. No critic, whatever her or his moldiness *or* skepticism, can evade a Nietzschean will to power over a text, because interpretation is at last nothing else. The text, even if it was written that morning, and shown by its poet to the critic at high noon, is already lost in time, as lost as the Yahwist. Time says, "It was," and authentic criticism, as Nietzsche implied, is necessarily pervaded by a will for revenge against time's "it was." No interpreter can suspend the will to relational knowledge for more than an isolated moment, and since all narrative and all poetry are also interpretation, all writing manifests such a will.

Solomon the King, nowhere of course overtly mentioned by J, is the dominant contemporary force in the context of J's writing. I would go further, and as a pious Stevensian would say that Solomon is J's motive for metaphor. The reign of Solomon ended in the year 922 before the Common Era, and J quite possibly wrote either in Solomon's last years, or—more likely, I think—shortly thereafter. One can venture that Solomon was to J what Elizabeth was to Shakespeare, an idea of order, as crucial in J's Jerusalem as it was in Shakespeare's London. The Imperial Theme is J's countersong, though J's main burden is a heroic and agonistic past represented by David the King, while his implied judgment upon the imperial present is at best skeptical, since he implies also an agonistic future. J's vision of agon centers his uncanny stance, accounting for his nearly unique mode of irony.

How much of J's actual text we have lost to the replacement tactics of redactors we cannot know, but biblical scholarship has not persuaded me that either the so-called Elohistic or the Priestly redactors provide fully coherent visions of their own, except perhaps for the Priestly first chapter of Genesis, which is so startling a contrast to J's account of how we all got started. But let me sketch the main contours of J's narrative, as we appear to have it. Yahweh begins his Creation in the first harsh Judean spring, before the first rain comes down. Water wells up from the earth, and Yahweh molds Adam out of the red clay, breathing into the earthling's nostrils a breath of the divine life. Then come the stories we think we know: Eve, the serpent, Cain and Abel, Seth, Noah and the Flood, the tower of Babel, and something utterly new with Abraham. From Abraham on, the main sequence again belongs to J: the Covenant, Ishmael, Yahweh at Mamre and on the road to Sodom, Lot, Isaac and the Akedah, Rebecca, Esau and Jacob, the tales of Jacob, Tamar, the story of Joseph and his brothers, and then the Mosaic account. Moses, so far as I can tell, meant much less to J than he did to the normative redactors, and so the J strand in Exodus and Numbers is even more laconic than J tended to be earlier.

In J's Exodus we find the oppression of the Jews, the birth of Moses, his escape to Midian, the burning bush and the instruction, the weird murderous attack by Yahweh upon Moses, the audiences with Pharaoh, the plagues, and the departure, flight, and crossing. Matters become sparser with Israel in the wilderness, at the Sinai covenant, and then with the dissensions and the battles in Numbers. J flares up finally on a grand scale in the serio-comic Balaam and Balak episode, but that is not the end of J's work, even as we have it. The Deuteronomist memorably incorporates J in his chapters 31 and 34, dealing with the death of Moses. I give here in sequence the opening and the close of what we hear J's Yahweh speaking aloud, first to Adam and last to Moses: "Of every tree in the garden you are free to eat; but as for the tree of knowledge of good and bad, you must not eat of it; for as soon as you eat of it, you shall die." "This is the land of which I swore to Abraham, Isaac, and Jacob, 'I will give it to your offspring.' I have let you see it with your own eyes, but you shall not cross there." Rhetorically, the two speeches share the same cruel pattern of power: "Here it is; it is yours and yet it is not yours." Akin to J's counterpointing of Yahweh's first and last speeches is his counterparting of Yahweh's first and last actions: "Yahweh formed man from the dust of the earth," and "Yahweh buried him, Moses, in the valley in the land of Moab, near Beth-peor; and no one knows his burial place to this day." From Adam to Moses is from earth to earth; Yahweh molds us and he buries us, and both actions are done with his own hands. As it was with Adam and Moses, so it was with David and with Solomon, and with those who come and will come after Solomon. J is the harshest and most monitory of writers, and his Yahweh is an uncanny god, who takes away much of what he gives, and who is beyond any standard of measurement. And yet what I have said about J so far is not even part of the truth; isolated, all by itself, it is not true at all, for J is a writer who exalts man, and who has most peculiar relations with God. Gorky once said of Tolstoy that Tolstoy's relation to God reminded him of the Russian proverb "Two bears in one den." J's relation to his uncanny Yahweh frequently reminds me of my favorite Yiddish apothegm: "Sleep faster, we need the pillows." J barely can keep up with Yahweh, though J's Jacob almost can, while J's Moses cannot keep up at all. Since what is most problematic about J's writing is Yahweh, I suggest we take a closer look at J's Yahweh than the entire normative and modern scholarly tradition has been willing or able to take. Homer and Dante, Shakespeare and Milton hardly lacked audacity in representing what may be beyond representation, but J was both bolder and shrewder than any other writer at inventing speeches and actions for God Himself. Only J convinces us that he knows precisely how and when Yahweh speaks; Isaiah compares poorly to J in this, while the Milton of *Paradise Lost*, Book III, hardly rates even as an involuntary parodist of J.

I am moved to ask a question which the normative tradition—Judaic, Christian, and even secular—cannot ask: What is J's stance toward Yahweh? I can begin an answer by listing all that it is not: creating Yahweh, J's primary emotions do not include awe, fear, wonder, much surprise, or even love. J *sounds* rather matter-of-fact, but that is part of J's unique mode of irony. By turns, J's stance toward Yahweh is appreciative, wryly apprehensive, intensely interested, and above all attentive and alert. Toward Yahweh, J is perhaps a touch wary; J is always *prepared to be surprised*. What J knows is that Yahweh is Sublime or "uncanny," incommensurate yet rather agonistic, curious and lively, humorous yet irascible, and all too capable of suddenly violent action. But J's Yahweh is rather *heimlich* also; he sensibly avoids walking about in the Near Eastern heat, preferring the cool of the evening, and he likes to sit under the terebinths at Mamre, devouring roast calf and curds. J would have laughed at his normative descendants—Christian, Jewish, secular, scholarly—who go on calling his representations of Yahweh "anthropomorphic," when they should be calling his representations of Jacob "theomorphic."

"The anthropomorphic" always has been a misleading concept, and probably was the largest single element affecting the long history of the redaction of J that evolved into normative Judaism. Most modern scholars, Jewish and Gentile alike, cannot seem to accept the fact that there was no Jewish theology before Philo. "Jewish theology," despite its long history from Philo to Franz Rosenzweig, is therefore an oxymoron, particularly when applied to biblical texts, and most particularly when applied to J. J's Yahweh is an uncanny personality, and not at all a concept. Yahweh sometimes *seems* to behave like us, but because Yahweh and his sculpted creature, Adam, are incommensurate, this remains a mere seeming. Sometimes, and always within limits, we behave like Yahweh, and not necessarily because we will to do so. There is a true sense in which John Calvin was as strong a reader of J as he more clearly was of Job, a sense displayed in the paradox of the Protestant Yahweh who entraps his believers by an impossible double injunction, which might be phrased: "Be like me, but don't you dare to be too like me!" In J, the paradox emerges only gradually, and does not reach its climax until the theophany on Sinai. Until Sinai, J's Yahweh addresses himself only to a handful, to his elite: Adam, Noah, Abraham, Jacob, Joseph, and, by profound implication, David. But at Sinai, we encounter the crisis of J's writing, as we will see.

What is theomorphic about Adam, Noah, Abraham, Jacob, Joseph? I think the question should be rephrased: What is Davidic about them? About Joseph, everything, and indeed J's Joseph I read as a fictive representation of David, rather in the way Virgil's Divine Child represents Augustus, except that J is working on a grand scale with Joseph, bringing to perfection what may have been an old mode of romance.

I have called Solomon J's motive for metaphor, but that calling resounds with Nietzsche's motive for all trope: the desire to be different, the desire to be elsewhere. For J, the difference, the elsewhere, is David. J's agonistic elitism, the struggle for the blessing, is represented by Abraham, above all by Jacob, and by Tamar also. But the bearer of the blessing is David, and I have ventured the surmise that J's Joseph is a portrait of David. Though this surmise is, I think, original, the centering of J's humanism upon the implied figure of David is not, of course, original with me. It is a fundamental postulate of the school of Gerhard von Rad, worked out in detail by theologians like Hans Walter Wolff and Walter Brueggemann. Still, a phrase like Wolff's "the Kerygma of the Yahwist" makes me rather uneasy, since J is no more a theologian than he is a priest or prophet. Freud, like St. Paul, has a message, but J, like Shakespeare, does not. J *is* literature and not "confession," which of course is not true of his redactors. They were on the road to Akiba, but J, always in excess of the normative, was no quester.

I find no traces of cult in J, and I am puzzled that so many read as kerygmatic Yahweh's words to Abram in Gen. 12:3: "So, then, all the families of the earth can gain a blessing in you." The blessing, in J, simply does not mean what it came to mean in his redactors and in the subsequent normative tradition. To gain a blessing, particularly through the blessing that becomes Abraham's, is in J to join oneself to that elitest agon which culminated in the figure of the agonistic hero, David. To be blessed means ultimately that one's name will not be scattered, and the remembered name will retain life into a time without boundaries. The blessing then is temporal, and not spatial, as it was in Homer and in the Greeks after him, who like his heroes struggled for the foremost place. And a temporal blessing, like the kingdom in Shakespeare, finds its problematic aspect in the vicissitudes of descendants.

Jacob is J's central man, whose fruition, deferred in the beloved Joseph, because given to Judah, has come just before J's time in the triumph of David. I think that Brueggemann is imaginatively accurate in his hypothesis that David represented, for J, a new kind of man, almost a new Adam, the man whom Yahweh (in 2 Sam. 7) had decided to trust. Doubtless we cannot exclude from our considerations the Messianic tradition that the normative, Jewish and Christian, were to draw out from those two great contemporary writers, J and the author of 2 Samuel. But J does not have any such Messianic consciousness about David. Quite the reverse: for him, we can surmise, David had been and was the elite *image*; not a harbinger of a greater vision to come, but a fully human being who already had exhausted the full range and vitality of man's possibilities. If, as Brueggemann speculates, J's tropes of exile (Gen. 3:24, 4:12, 11:8) represent the true images of the Solomonic present, then I would find J's prime Davidic trope in Jacob's return to Canaan, marked by the all-night, all-in wrestling match that concentrates Jacob's name forever as Israel. The Davidic glory then is felt most strongly in Jacob's theomorphic triumph, rendered so much the more poignant by his permanent crippling: "The sun rose upon him as he passed Penuel, limping on his hip."

If Jacob is Israel as the father, then David, through the trope of Joseph, is Jacob's or Israel's truest son. What then is Davidic about J's Jacob? I like the late E. A. Speiser's surmise that J personally knew his great contemporary, the writer who gave us, in 2 Samuel, the history of David and his immediate successors. J's Joseph reads to me like a lovingly ironic parody of the David of the court historian. What matters most about David, as that model narrative presents him, is not only his charismatic intensity, but the marvelous gratuity of Yahweh's *hesed*, his Election-love for this most heroic of his favorites. To no one in J's text does Yahweh speak so undialectically as he does through Nathan to David in 2 Samuel 7:12–16:

> When your days are done and you lie with your fathers, I will raise
> up your offspring after you, one of your own issue, and I will establish
> his kingship. He shall build a house for My name, and I will establish
> his royal throne forever. I will be a father to him, and he shall be
> a son to Me. When he does wrong, I will chastise him with the
> rod of men and the affliction of mortals; but I will never withdraw
> My favor from him as I withdrew it from Saul, whom I removed
> to make room for you. Your house and your kingship shall ever be
> secure before you; your throne shall be established forever.

The blessing in J, as I have written elsewhere, is always agonistic, and Jacob is J's supreme agonist. But J makes a single exception for Joseph, and clearly with the reader's eye centered upon David. From the womb on to the ford of the Jabbok, Jacob is an agonist, and until that night encounter at Penuel by no means a heroic one. His agon, as I've said, is for the temporal blessing that will prevail into a time without boundaries; and so it never resembles the Homeric or the Athenian contest for the foremost place, a kind of topological or spatial blessing. In J, the struggle is for the uncanny gift of life, for the breath of Yahweh that transforms *adamah* into Adam. True, David struggles, and suffers, but J's Joseph serenely voyages through all vicissitudes, as though J were intimating that David's agon had been of a new kind, one in which the obligation was wholly and voluntarily on Yahweh's side in the Covenant. Jacob the father wrestles lifelong, and is permanently crippled by the climactic match with a nameless one among the Elohim whom I interpret as the baffled angel of death, who learns that Israel lives, and always will survive. Joseph the son charms reality, even as David seems to have charmed Yahweh.

But Jacob, I surmise, was J's signature, and while the portrait of the Davidic Joseph manifests J's wistfulness, the representation of Jacob may well be J's self-portrait as the great writer of Israel. My earlier question would then become: What is Davidic about J himself, not as a person perhaps, but certainly as an author? My first observation here would have to be this apparent paradox: J is anything but a religious writer, unlike all his revisionists and interpreters, and David is anything but a religious personality, despite having become the paradigm for all Messianic speculation, both Jewish and Christian. Again I am in the wake of von Rad and his school, but with this crucial Bloomian swerve: J and David are not religious, just as Freud, for all his avowedly antireligious polemic, is finally nothing but religious. Freud's overdetermination of meaning, his emphasis upon primal repression or a flight from representation—before, indeed, there was anything to represent—establishes Freud as normatively Jewish despite himself. Turn it and turn it, for everything is in it, the sage ben Bag Bag said of Torah, and Freud says the same of the psyche. If there is sense in everything, then everything that is going to happen has happened already, and so reality is already in the past and there never can be anything new. Freud's stance toward psychic history is the normative rabbinical stance toward Jewish history, and if Akiba is the paradigm for what it is to be religious, then the professedly scientistic Freud is as religious as Akiba, if we are speaking of the Jewish religion. But J, like the court historian's David of 2 Samuel, is quite Jewish without being at all religious, in the belated normative sense. For the uncanny J, and for the path-breaking David, everything that matters most is perpetually new.

But this is true of J's Jacob also, as it is of Abraham, even Isaac, and certainly Tamar—all live at the edge of life rushing onwards, never in a static present but always in the dynamism of J's Yahweh, whose incessant temporality generates anxious expectations in nearly every fresh sentence of certain passages. This is again the Kafkan aspect of J, though it is offset by J's strong sense of human freedom, a sense surpassing its Homeric parallels. What becomes theodicy in J's revisionists down to Milton is for J not at all a perplexity. Since J has no concept of Yahweh but rather a sense of Yahweh's peculiar personality, the interventions of Yahweh in primal family history do not impinge upon his elite's individual freedom. So we have the memorable and grimly funny argument between Yahweh and Abraham as they walk together down the road to Sodom. Abraham wears Yahweh down until Yahweh quite properly begins to get exasperated. The shrewd courage and humanity of Abraham convince me that in the Akedah the redactors simply eliminated J's text almost completely. As I read the Hebrew, there is an extraordinary gap between the Elohistic language and the sublime invention of the story. J's Abraham would have argued far more tenaciously with Yahweh for his son's life than he did in defense of the inhabitants of the sinful cities of the plain, and here the revisionists may have defrauded us of J's uncanny greatness at its height.

But how much they *have* left us which the normative tradition has been incapable of assimilating! I think the best way of seeing this is to juxtapose with J the Pharasaic Book of Jubilees, oddly called also "the Little Genesis," though it is prolix and redundant in every tiresome way. Written about one hundred years before the Common Era, Jubilees is a normative travesty of Genesis, far more severely, say, than Chronicles is a normative reduction of 2 Samuel. But though he writes so boringly, what is wonderfully illuminating about the author of Jubilees is that he totally eradicates J's text. Had he set out deliberately to remove everything idiosyncratic about J's share in Torah, he could have done no more thorough a job. Gone altogether is J's creation story of Yahweh molding the red clay into Adam and then breathing life into his own image. Gone as well is Yahweh at Mamre, where only angels now appear to Abraham and Sarah, and there is no dispute on the road to Sodom. And the Satanic prince of angels, Mastema, instigates Yahweh's trial of Abraham in the Akedah. Jacob and Esau do not wrestle in the womb, and Abraham prefers Jacob, though even the author of Jubilees does not go so far as to deny Isaac's greater love for Esau. Gone, alas totally gone, is J's sublime invention of the night wrestling at Penuel. Joseph lacks all charm and mischief, necessarily, and the agony of Jacob, and the subsequent grandeur of the reunion, are vanished away. Most revealingly, the uncanniest moment in J, Yahweh's attempt to murder Moses en route to Egypt, becomes Mastema's act. And wholly absent is J's most enigmatic vision, the Sinai theophany, which is replaced by the safe removal of J's too-lively Yahweh back to a sedate dwelling in the high heavens.

J's originality was too radical to be absorbed, and yet abides even now as the originality of a Yahweh who will not dwindle down into the normative Godhead of the Jews, Christians, and Muslims. Because J cared more for personality than for morality, and cared not at all for cult, his legacy is a disturbing sense that, as Blake phrased it, forms of worship have been chosen from poetic tales. J was no theologian and yet not a maker of saga or epic, and again not a historian, and not even a storyteller as such. We have no description of J that will fit, just as we have no idea of God that will contain his irrepressible Yahweh.

The Sacrifice of Isaac

Erich Auerbach

The genius of the Homeric style becomes [especially] apparent when it is compared with an equally ancient and equally epic style from a different world of forms. I shall attempt this comparison with the account of the sacrifice of Isaac, a homogeneous narrative produced by the so-called Elohist. The King James version translates the opening as follows (Gen. 22:1): "And it came to pass after these things, that God did tempt Abraham, and said to him, Abraham! and he said, Behold, here I am." Even this opening startles us when we come to it from Homer. Where are the two speakers? We are not told. The reader, however, knows that they are not normally to be found together in one place on earth, that one of them, God, in order to speak to Abraham, must come from somewhere, must enter the earthly realm from some unknown heights or depths. Whence does he come, whence does he call to Abraham? We are not told. He does not come, like Zeus or Poseidon, from the Aethiopians, where he has been enjoying a sacrificial feast. Nor are we told anything of his reasons for tempting Abraham so terribly. He has not, like Zeus, discussed them in set speeches with other gods gathered in council; nor have the deliberations in his own heart been presented to us; unexpected and mysterious, he enters the scene from some unknown height or depth and calls: Abraham! It will at once be said that this is to be explained by the particular concept of God which the Jews held and which was wholly different from that of the Greeks. True enough—but this constitutes no objection. For how is the Jewish concept of God to be explained? Even their earlier God of the desert was not fixed in form and content, and was alone; his lack of form, his lack of local habitation, his singleness, was in the

From *Mimesis: The Representation of Reality in Western Literature*. Translated by Willard R. Traski. © 1953, © 1981 renewed by Princeton University Press.

end not only maintained but developed even further in competition with the comparatively far more manifest gods of the surrounding Near Eastern world. The concept of God held by the Jews is less a cause than a symptom of their manner of comprehending and representing things.

This becomes still clearer if we now turn to the other person in the dialogue, to Abraham. Where is he? We do not know. He says, indeed: Here I am—but the Hebrew word means only something like "behold me," and in any case is not meant to indicate the actual place where Abraham is, but a moral position in respect to God, who has called to him—Here am I awaiting thy command. Where he is actually, whether in Beersheba or elsewhere, whether indoors or in the open air, is not stated; it does not interest the narrator, the reader is not informed; and what Abraham was doing when God called to him is left in the same obscurity. To realize the difference, consider Hermes' visit to Calypso, for example, where command, journey, arrival and reception of the visitor, situation and occupation of the person visited, are set forth in many verses; and even on occasions when gods appear suddenly and briefly, whether to help one of their favorites or to deceive or destroy some mortal whom they hate, their bodily forms, and usually the manner of their coming and going, are given in detail. Here, however, God appears without bodily form (yet he "appears"), coming from some unspecified place—we only hear his voice, and that utters nothing but a name, a name without an adjective, without a descriptive epithet for the person spoken to, such as is the rule in every Homeric address; and of Abraham too nothing is made perceptible except the words in which he answers God: *Hinne-ni*, Behold me here—with which, to be sure, a most touching gesture expressive of obedience and readiness is suggested, but it is left to the reader to visualize it. Moreover the two speakers are not on the same level: if we conceive of Abraham in the foreground, where it might be possible to picture him as prostrate or kneeling or bowing with outspread arms or gazing upward, God is not there too: Abraham's words and gestures are directed toward the depths of the picture or upward, but in any case the undetermined, dark place from which the voice comes to him is not in the foreground.

After this opening, God gives his command, and the story itself begins: everyone knows it; it unrolls with no episodes in a few independent sentences whose syntactical connection is of the most rudimentary sort. In this atmosphere it is unthinkable that an implement, a landscape through which the travelers passed, the serving-men, or the ass, should be described, that their origin or descent or material or appearance or usefulness should be set forth in terms of praise; they do not even admit an adjective: they are serving-men, ass, wood, and knife, and nothing else, without an epithet; they are there to serve the end which God has commanded; what in other respects they were, are, or will be, remains in darkness. A journey is made, because God has designated the place where the sacrifice is to be performed; but we are told nothing about the journey except that it took three days, and even that we are told in a mysterious way: Abraham and his followers rose "early in the morning" and "went unto" the place of which God had told him; on the third day he lifted up his eyes and saw the place from afar. That gesture is the only gesture, is indeed the only occurrence during the whole journey, of which we are told; and though its motivation lies in the fact that the place is elevated, its uniqueness still heightens the impression that the journey took place through a vacuum; it is as if, while he traveled on, Abraham had looked neither to the right nor to the left, had suppressed any sign of life in his followers and himself save only their footfalls.

Thus the journey is like a silent progress through the indeterminate and the contingent, a holding of the breath, a process which has no present, which is inserted, like a blank duration, between what has passed and what lies ahead, and which yet is measured: three days! Three such days positively demand the symbolic interpretation which they later received. They began "early in the morning." But at what time on the third day did Abraham lift up his eyes and see his goal? The text says nothing on the subject. Obviously not "late in the evening," for it seems that there was still time enough to climb the mountain and make the sacrifice. So "early in the morning" is given, not as an indication of time, but for the sake of its ethical significance; it is intended to express the resolution, the promptness, the punctual obedience of the sorely tried Abraham. Bitter to him is the early morning in which he saddles his ass, calls his serving-men and his son Isaac, and sets out; but he obeys, he walks on until the third day, then lifts up his eyes and sees the place. Whence he comes, we do not know, but the goal is clearly stated: Jeruel in the land of Moriah. What place this is meant to indicate is not clear—"Moriah" especially may be a later correction of some other word. But in any case the goal was given, and in any case it is a matter of some sacred spot which was to receive a particular consecration by being connected with Abraham's sacrifice. Just as little as "early in the morning" serves as a temporal indication does "Jeruel in the land of Moriah" serve as a geographical indication; and in both cases alike, the complementary indication is not given, for we know as little of the hour at which Abraham lifted up his eyes as we do of the place from which he set forth—Jeruel is significant not so much as the goal of an earthly journey, in its geographical relation to other places, as through its special election, through its relation to God, who designated it as the scene of the act, and therefore it must be named.

In the narrative itself, a third chief character appears: Isaac. While God and Abraham, the serving-men, the ass, and the implements are simply named, without mention of any qualities or any other sort of definition, Isaac once receives an appositive; God says, "Take Isaac, thine only son, whom thou lovest." But this is not a characterization of Isaac as a person, apart from his relation to his father and apart from the story; he may be handsome or ugly, intelligent or stupid, tall or short, pleasant or unpleasant — we are not told. Only what we need to know about him as a personage in the action, here and now, is illuminated, so that it may become apparent how terrible Abraham's temptation is, and that God is fully aware of it. By this example of the contrary, we see the significance of the descriptive adjectives and digressions of the Homeric poems; with their indications of the earlier and as it were absolute existence of the persons described, they prevent the reader from concentrating exclusively on a present crisis; even when the most terrible things are occurring, they prevent the establishment of an overwhelming suspense. But here, in the story of Abraham's sacrifice, the overwhelming suspense is present; what Schiller makes the goal of the tragic poet — to rob us of our emotional freedom, to turn our intellectual and spiritual powers (Schiller says "our activity") in one direction, to concentrate them there — is effected in this Biblical narrative, which certainly deserves the epithet epic.

We find the same contrast if we compare the two uses of direct discourse. The personages speak in the Bible story too; but their speech does not serve, as does speech in Homer, to manifest, to externalize thoughts — on the contrary, it serves to indicate thoughts which remain unexpressed. God gives his command in direct discourse, but he leaves his motives and his purpose unexpressed; Abraham, receiving the command, says nothing and does what he has been told to do. The conversation between Abraham and Isaac on the way to the place of sacrifice is only an interruption of the heavy silence and makes it all the more burdensome. The two of them, Isaac carrying the wood and Abraham with fire and a knife, "went together." Hesitantly, Isaac ventures to ask about the ram, and Abraham gives the well-known answer. Then the text repeats: "So they went both of them together." Everything remains unexpressed.

It would be difficult, then, to imagine styles more contrasted than those of these two equally ancient and equally epic texts. On the one hand, externalized, uniformly illuminated phenomena, at a definite time and in a definite place, connected together without lacunae in a perpetual foreground; thoughts and feeling completely expressed; events taking place in leisurely fashion and with very little of suspense. On the other hand, the externalization of only so much of the phenomena as is necessary for the purpose of the narrative, all else left in obscurity; the decisive points of the narrative alone are emphasized, what lies between is nonexistent; time and place are undefined and call for interpretation; thoughts and feeling remain unexpressed, are only suggested by the silence and the fragmentary speeches; the whole, permeated with the most unrelieved suspense and directed toward a single goal (and to that extent far more of a unity), remains mysterious and "fraught with background."

I will discuss this term in some detail, lest it be misunderstood. I said [elsewhere] that the Homeric style was "of the foreground" because, despite much going back and forth, it yet causes what is momentarily being narrated to give the impression that it is the only present, pure and without perspective. A consideration of the Elohistic text teaches us that our term is capable of a broader and deeper application. It shows that even the separate personages can be represented as possessing "background"; God is always so represented in the Bible, for he is not comprehensible in his presence, as is Zeus; it is always only "something" of him that appears, he always extends into depths. But even the human beings in the biblical stories have greater depths of time, fate, and consciousness than do the human beings in Homer; although they are nearly always caught up in an event engaging all their faculties, they are not so entirely immersed in its present that they do not remain continually conscious of what has happened to them earlier and elsewhere; their thoughts and feelings have more layers, are more entangled. Abraham's actions are explained not only by what is happening to him at the moment, nor yet only by his character (as Achilles' actions by his courage and his pride, and Odysseus's by his versatility and foresightedness), but by his previous history; he remembers, he is constantly conscious of, what God has promised him and what God has already accomplished for him—his soul is torn between desperate rebellion and hopeful expectation; his silent obedience is multilayered, has background. Such a problematic psychological situation as this is impossible for any of the Homeric heroes, whose destiny is clearly defined and who wake every morning as if it were the first day of their lives: their emotions, though strong, are simple and find expression instantly.

The First Three Chapters of Genesis: Principles of Governance Stated Narratively

Kenneth Burke

Imagine that you wanted to say, "The world can be divided into six major classifications." That is, you wanted to deal with "the principles of Order," beginning with the natural order, and placing man's socio-political order with reference to it. But you wanted to treat of these matters in *narrative* terms, which necessarily involve *temporal* sequence (in contrast with the cycle of terms for "Order" that merely cluster about one another, variously implying one another, but in no one fixed sequence).

Stated narratively (in the style of Genesis, *Bereshith*, Beginning), such an idea of principles, or "firsts" would not be stated simply in terms of classification, as were we to say "The first of six primary classes would be such-and-such, the second such-and-such" and so on. Rather, a completely narrative style would properly translate the idea of six classes or categories into terms of time, as were we to assign each of the classes to a separate "day." Thus, instead of saying "And that completes the first broad division, or classification, of our subject-matter," we'd say: "And the evening and the morning were the first day" (or, more accurately, the "One" Day). And so on, through the six broad classes, ending "last but not least," on the category of man and his dominion.

Further, a completely narrative style would *personalize* the principle of classification. This role is performed by the references to God's creative fiat, which from the very start infuses the sheerly natural order with the verbal principle

From *The Rhetoric of Religion: Studies in Logology.* © 1970 by The Regents of the University of California. University of California Press, 1970.

(the makings of that "reason" which we take to be so essential an aspect of human personality).

Logologically, the statement that God made man in his image would be translated as: The principle of personality implicit in the idea of the first creative fiats, whereby all things are approached in terms of the word, applies also to the feeling for symbol-systems on the part of the human animal, who would come to read nature as if it were a book. Insofar as God's words infused the natural order with their genius, and insofar as God is represented as speaking words to the first man and woman, the principle of human personality (which is at the very start identified with *dominion*) has its analogue in the notion of God as a super-person, and of nature as the act of such a super-agent. (That is, we take symbol-using to be a distinctive ingredient of "personality.")

Though technically there is a kind of "proto-fall" implicit in the principle of divisiveness that characterizes the Bible's view of the Creation, and though the principle of subjection is already present (in the general outlines of a government with God at its head, and mankind as subject to His authority while in turn having dominion over all else in the natural realm), the Covenant (as first announced in the first chapter) is necessarily Edenic, in a state of "innocence," since no negative command has yet been pronounced. From the dialectical point of view (in line with the Order-Disorder pair) we may note that there is a possibility of "evil" implicit in the reference to all six primary classifications as "good." But in all three points (the divisiveness, the order of dominion, and the universal goodness) the explicit negative is lacking. In fact, the nearest approach to an outright negative (and that not of a moralistic, hortatory sort) is in the reference to the "void" (*bohu*) which preceded God's classificatory acts. Rashi says that the word translated as "formless" (*tohu*) "has the meaning of astonishment and amazement." Incidentally, in connection with Gen. 1:29, *The Interpreter's Bible* suggests another implicit negative, in that the explicit permitting of a vegetarian diet implies that Adam may *not* eat flesh.

In the first chapter of Genesis, the stress is upon the creative fiat as a means of classification. It says in effect, "What hath God wrought (by his Word)?" The second chapter's revised account of the Creation shifts the emphasis to matters of dominion, saying in effect, "What hath God ordained (by his Words)?" The seventh "day" (or category), which is placed at the beginning of the second chapter, has a special dialectical interest in its role as a transition between the two emphases.

In one sense, the idea of the Sabbath is implicitly a negative, being conceived as antithetical to all the six foregoing categories, which are classifiable together under the single head of "work," in contrast with this seventh category, of "rest." That is, work and rest are "polar" terms, dialectical opposites. (In his *Politics,* Aristotle's terms bring out this negative relation explicitly, since his word for business activity is *ascholein,* that is, "*not* to be at leisure," though we should tend rather to use the negative the other way round, defining "rest" as "not to be at work.")

This seventh category (of rest after toil) obviously serves well as transition between Order (of God as principle of origination) and Order (of God as principle of sovereignty). *Leisure* arises as an "institution" only when conditions of dominion have regularized the patterns of *work.* And fittingly, just after this transitional passage, the very name of God undergoes a change (the quality of which is well indicated in our translations by a shift from "God" to "Lord God." Here, whereas in Gen. 1:29, *God* tells the man and woman that the fruit of "every tree" is permitted them, the *Lord God* (Gen. 2:17) notably revises thus: "But of the tree of the knowledge of good and evil, thou shalt not eat of it: for in the day that thou eatest thereof thou shalt surely die." Here, with the stress upon governance, enters the negative of command.

When, later, the serpent tempts "the woman" (Gen. 3:4), saying that "Ye shall not surely die," his statement is proved partially correct, to the extent that they did not die on the day on which they ate of the forbidden fruit. In any case, Gen. 3:19 pronounces the formula that has been theologically interpreted as deriving mankind's physical death from our first parents' first disobedience: "In the sweat of thy face shalt thou eat bread, till thou return unto the ground; for out of it wast thou taken: for dust thou art, and unto dust shalt thou return."

The Interpreter's Bible denies there is any suggestion that man would have lived forever had he not eaten of the forbidden fruit. Gen. 3:20 is taken to imply simply that man would have regarded death as his natural end, rather than as "the last fearful frustration." Thus, the fear of death is said to be "the consequence of the disorder in man's relationships," when they are characterized "by domination" (along with the fear that the subject will break free of their subjection). This seems to be at odds with the position taken by the Scofield Bible which, in the light of Paul's statements in Rom. 5:12–21 ("by one man sin entered the world, and death by sin"—and "by one man's offence death reigned by one") interprets the passage as meaning that "physical death" is due to a "universal sinful *state,* or nature" which is "our heritance from Adam."

It is within neither our present purpose nor our competency to interpret this verse theologically. But here's how it would look logologically:

First, we would note that in referring to "disorder" and "domination," *The Interpreter's Bible* is but referring to "Order" and "Dominion," as seen from another angle. For a mode of domination is a mode of dominion; and a socio-political order is by nature a ziggurat-like structure which, as the story of the Tower makes obvious, can stand for the principle of Disorder.

If we are right in our notion that the idea of Mortification is integral to the idea of Dominion (as the scrupulous subject must seek to "slay" within himself whatever impulses run counter to the authoritative demands of sovereignty), then all about a story of the "first" dominion and the "first" disobedience there should hover the theme of the "first" mortification.

But "mortification" is a weak term, as compared with "death." And thus, in the essentializing ways proper to the narrative style, this stronger, more dramatic term replaces the weaker, more "philosophic" one. "Death" would be the proper narrative-dramatic way of saying "Mortification." By this arrangement, the natural order is once again seen through the eyes of the socio-political order, as the idea of mortification in the toil and subjection of Governance is replaced by the image of death in nature.

From the standpoint sheerly of imagery (once the idea of mortification has been reduced to the idea of death, and the idea of death has been reduced to the image of a dead body rotting back into the ground), we now note a kind of "imagistic proto-fall," in the pun of Gen. 2:7, where the Lord God is shown creating man (*adham*) out of the ground (*adhamah*). Here would be an imagistic way of saying that man in his physical nature is essentially but earth, the sort of thing a body becomes when it decays; or that man is *first of all* but earth, as regards his place in the sheerly natural order. You'd define in narrative or temporal terms by showing what he came from. But insofar as he is what he came from, then such a definition would be completed in narrative terms by the image of his return to his origins. In this sense, the account of man's forming (in Gen. 2:7) ambiguously lays the conditions for his "return" to such origins, as the Lord God makes explicit in Gen. 3:19, when again the subject is the relation between *adham* and the *adhamah:* "For dust thou art, and unto dust shalt thou return." Here would be a matter of sheer imagistic consistency, for making the stages of a narrative be all of one piece.

But the death motif here is explicitly related to another aspect of Order or Dominion: the sweat of toil. And looking back a bit further, we find that this severe second Covenant (the "Adamic") also subjected woman to the rule of the husband—another aspect of Dominion. And there is to be an eternal enmity between man and the serpent (the image, or narrative personification, of the principle of Temptation, which we have also found to be intrinsic to the motives clustering about the idea of Order).

Logologically, then, the narrative would seem to be saying something like this: Even if you begin by thinking of death as a merely natural phenomenon, once you come to approach it in terms of conscience-laden *mortification* you get a new slant on it. For death then becomes seen, in terms of the socio-political order, as a kind of *capital punishment*. But something of so eschatological a nature is essentially a "first" (since "ends," too, are principles—and here is a place at which firsts and lasts meet, so far as narrative terms for the defining of essences are concerned). Accordingly death in the natural order becomes conceived as the fulfillment or completion of mortification in the socio-political order, but with the difference that, as with capital punishment in the sentencing of transgressions against sovereignty, it is not in itself deemed wholly "redemptive," since it needs further modifications, along the lines of placement in an undying Heavenly Kingdom after death. And this completes the pattern of Order: the symmetry of the socio-political (*cum* verbal), the natural, and the supernatural.

The Beginning of the Bible and Its Greek Counterparts

Leo Strauss

All the hopes that we entertain in the midst of the confusions and dangers of the present are founded positively or negatively, directly or indirectly on the experiences of the past. Of these experiences the broadest and deepest, as far as we Western men are concerned, are indicated by the names of the two cities Jerusalem and Athens. Western man became what he is and is what he is through the coming together of biblical faith and Greek thought. In order to understand ourselves and to illuminate our trackless way into the future, we must understand Jerusalem and Athens. As goes without saying, this is a task whose proper performance goes much beyond my power. . . . But we cannot define our tasks by our powers, for our powers become known to us through performing our tasks; it is better to fail nobly than to succeed basely. . . .

The objects to which we refer by speaking of Jerusalem and Athens, are today understood by the science devoted to such objects as cultures; "culture" is meant to be a scientific concept. According to this concept there is an indefinitely large number of cultures: *n* cultures. The scientist who studies them beholds them as objects; as scientist he stands outside of all of them; he has no preference for any of them; in his eyes all of them are of equal rank; he is not only impartial but objective; he is anxious not to distort any of them; in speaking about them he avoids any "culture-bound" concepts, i.e., concepts bound to any particular culture or kind of culture. In many cases the objects studied by the scientist of culture do or did not know that they are or were cultures. This causes no difficulty for him: electrons also do not know that they are electrons; even dogs do not know that they are dogs. By the mere fact that he speaks of his objects as cultures,

From *Jerusalem and Athens: Some Preliminary Reflections* (City College Papers, no. 6). © 1967 by The City College of the City University of New York.

the scientific student takes it for granted that he understands the people whom he studies better than they understood or understand themselves.

This whole approach has been questioned for some time but this questioning does not seem to have had any effect on the scientists. The man who started the questioning was Nietzsche. We have said that according to the prevailing view there were or are *n* cultures. Let us say there were or are 1,001 cultures, thus reminding ourselves of the Arabian Nights, the 1,001 Nights; the account of the cultures, if it is well done will be a series of exciting stories, perhaps of tragedies. Accordingly Nietzsche speaks of our subject in a speech of his Zarathustra that is entitled "Of 1,000 Goals and One." The Hebrews and the Greeks appear in this speech as two among a number of nations, not superior to the two others that are mentioned or to the 996 that are not mentioned. The peculiarity of the Greeks is the full dedication of the individual to the contest for excellence, distinction, supremacy. The peculiarity of the Hebrews is the utmost honoring of father and mother. (Up to this day the Jews read on their highest holiday the section of the Torah that deals with the first presupposition of honoring father and mother: the unqualified prohibition against incest between children and parents.) Nietzsche has a deeper reverence than any other beholder for the sacred tables of the Hebrews as well as of the other nations in question. Yet since he is only a beholder of these tables, since what one table commends or commands is incompatible with what the others command, he is not subject to the commandments of any. This is true also and especially of the tables, or "values" of modern Western culture. But according to him, all scientific concepts, and hence in particular the concept of culture, are culture-bound; the concept of culture is an outgrowth of 19th century Western culture; its application to "cultures" of other ages and climates is an act stemming from the spiritual imperialism of that particular culture. There is then a glaring contradiction between the claimed objectivity of the science of cultures and the radical subjectivity of that science. Differently stated, one cannot behold, i.e., truly understand, any culture unless one is firmly rooted in one's own culture or unless one belongs in one's capacity as a beholder to some culture. But if the universality of the beholding of all cultures is to be preserved, the culture to which the beholder of all cultures belongs, must be the universal culture, the culture of mankind, the world culture; the universality of beholding presupposes, if only by anticipating it, the universal culture which is no longer one culture among many. The variety of cultures that have hitherto emerged contradicts the oneness of truth. Truth is not a woman so that each man can have his own truth as he can have his own wife. Nietzsche sought therefore for a culture that would no longer be particular and hence in the last analysis arbitrary. The single goal of mankind is conceived by him as in a sense superhuman: he speaks of the superman of the future. The superman is meant to unite in himself Jerusalem and Athens on the highest level.

However much the science of all cultures may protest its innocence of all preferences or evaluations it fosters a specific moral posture. Since it requires openness to all cultures, it fosters universal tolerance and the exhilaration deriving from the beholding of diversity; it necessarily affects all cultures that it can still affect by contributing to their transformation in one and the same direction; it willy-nilly brings about a shift of emphasis from the particular to the universal: by asserting, if only implicitly, the rightness of pluralism, it asserts that pluralism is *the* right way; it asserts the monism of universal tolerance and respect for diversity; for by virtue of being an -ism, pluralism is a monism.

One remains somewhat closer to the science of culture as commonly practiced if one limits oneself to saying that every attempt to understand the phenomena in question remains dependent on a conceptual framework that is alien to most of these phenomena and therefore necessarily distorts them. "Objectivity" can be expected only if one attempts to understand the various cultures or peoples exactly as they understand or understood themselves. Men of ages and climates other than our own did not understand themselves in terms of cultures because they were not concerned with culture in the present-day meaning of the term. What we now call culture is the accidental result of concerns that were not concerns with culture but with other things and above all with the Truth.

Yet our intention to speak of Jerusalem and Athens seems to compel us to go beyond the self-understanding of either. Or is there a notion, a word that points to the highest that the Bible on the one hand and the greatest works of the Greeks claim to convey? There is such a word: wisdom. Not only the Greek philosophers but the Greek poets as well were considered to be wise men, and the Torah is said in the Torah to be "your wisdom in the eyes of the nations." We must then try to understand the difference between biblical wisdom and Greek wisdom. We see at once that each of the two claims to be the true wisdom, thus denying to the other its claim to be wisdom in the strict and highest sense. According to the Bible, the beginning of wisdom is fear of the Lord; according to the Greek philosophers, the beginning of wisdom is wonder. We are thus compelled from the very beginning to make a choice, to take a stand. Where then do we stand? We are confronted with the incompatible claims of Jerusalem and Athens to our allegiance. We are open to both and willing to listen to each. We ourselves are not wise but we wish to become wise. We are seekers for wisdom, *philo-sophoi*. By saying that we wish to hear first and then to act to decide, we have already decided in favor of Athens against Jerusalem.

This seems to be necessary for all of us who cannot be orthodox and therefore must accept the principle of the historical-critical study of the Bible. The Bible was traditionally understood as the true and authentic account of the deeds of God and men from the beginning till the restoration after the Babylonian exile. The deeds of God include His legislation as well as His inspirations of the prophets, and the deeds of men include their praises of God and their prayers to Him as well as their God-inspired admonitions. Biblical criticism starts from the observation that the biblical account is in important respects not authentic but derivative or consists not of "histories" but of "memories of ancient histories," to borrow a Machiavellian expression. Biblical criticism reached its first climax in Spinoza's *Theological-Political Treatise,* which is frankly anti-theological; Spinoza read the Bible as he read the Talmud and the Koran. The result of his criticism can be summarized as follows: the Bible consists to a considerable extent of self-contradictory assertions, of remnants of ancient prejudices or superstitions, and of the outpourings of an uncontrolled imagination; in addition it is poorly compiled and poorly preserved. He arrived at this result by presupposing the impossibility of miracles. The considerable differences between nineteenth- and twentieth-century biblical criticism and that of Spinoza can be traced to their difference in regard to the evaluation of imagination: whereas for Spinoza imagination is simply sub-rational, it was assigned a much higher rank in later times; it was understood as the vehicle of religious or spiritual experience, which necessarily expresses itself in symbols and the like. The historical-critical study of the Bible is the attempt to understand the various layers of the Bible as they were understood by their immediate addressees, i.e., the contemporaries of the authors of the various layers. The Bible speaks of many things that for the biblical authors themselves belong to the remote past; it suffices to mention the creation of the world. But there is undoubtedly much of history in the Bible, i.e., accounts of events written by contemporaries or near-contemporaries. One is thus led to say that the Bible contains both "myth" and "history." Yet this distinction is alien to the Bible; it is a special form of the distinction between *mythos* and *logos; mythos* and *historie* are of Greek origin. From the point of view of the Bible the "myths" are as true as the "histories": what Israel "in fact" did or suffered cannot be understood except in the light of the "facts" of Creation and Election. What is now called "historical" is those deeds and speeches that are equally accessible to the believer and to the unbeliever. But from the point of view of the Bible the unbeliever is the fool who has said in his heart "there is no God"; the Bible narrates everything as it is credible to the wise in the biblical sense of wisdom. Let us never forget that there is no biblical word for doubt. The biblical signs and wonders convince men who have little faith or who believe in other gods; they are not addressed to "the fools who say in their hearts 'there is no God.' "

It is true that we cannot ascribe to the Bible the theological concept of miracles, for that concept presupposes that of nature and the concept of nature is foreign to the Bible. One is tempted to ascribe to the Bible what one may call the poetic concept of miracles as illustrated by Psalm 114: "When Israel went out of Egypt, the house of Jacob from a people of strange tongue, Judah became his sanctuary and Israel his dominion. The sea saw and it fled; the Jordan turned back. The mountains skipped like rams, the hills like lambs. What ails thee, sea, that thou fleest, thou Jordan that thou turnst back? Ye mountains that ye skip like rams, ye hills like lambs? From the presence of the Lord tremble thou earth, from the presence of the God of Jacob who turns the rock into a pond of water, the flint into a fountain of waters." The presence of God or His call elicits a conduct of His creatures that differs strikingly from their ordinary conduct; it enlivens the lifeless; it makes fluid the fixed. It is not easy to say whether the author of the psalm did not mean his utterance to be simply or literally true. It is easy to say that the concept of poetry—as distinguished from that of song—is foreign to the Bible. It is perhaps more simple to say that owing to the victory of science over natural theology the impossibility of miracles can no longer be said to be simply true but has degenerated to the status of an indemonstrable hypothesis. One may trace to the hypothetical character of this fundamental premise the hypothetical character of many, not to say all, results of biblical criticism. Certain it is that biblical criticism in all its forms makes use of terms having no biblical equivalents and is to this extent unhistorical.

How then must we proceed? We shall not take issue with the findings and even the premises of biblical criticism. Let us grant that the Bible and in particular the Torah consists to a considerable extent of "memories of ancient histories," even of memories of memories; but memories of memories are not necessarily distorting or pale reflections of the original; they may be recollections of recollections, deepenings through meditation of the primary experiences. We shall therefore take the latest and uppermost layer as seriously as the earlier ones. We shall start from the uppermost layer—from what is first for us, even though it may not be the first simply. We shall start, that is, where both the traditional and the historical study of the Bible necessarily start. In thus proceeding we avoid the compulsion to make an advance decision in favor of Athens against Jerusalem. For the Bible does not require us to believe in the miraculous character of events that the Bible does not present as miraculous. God's speaking to men may be described as miraculous, but the Bible does not claim that the putting together of those speeches was done miraculously. We begin at the beginning, at the beginning of the beginning. The beginning of the beginning happens to deal with *the* beginning: the creation of heaven and earth. The Bible begins reasonably.

"In the beginning God created heaven and earth." Who says this? We are not told; hence we do not know. Does it make no difference who says it? This would be a philosopher's reason; is it also the biblical reason? We are not told; hence we do not know. We have no right to assume that God said it, for the Bible introduces God's sayings by expressions like "God said." We shall then assume that the words were spoken by a nameless man. Yet no man can have been an eyewitness of God's creating heaven and earth; the only eyewitness was God. Since "there did not arise in Israel a prophet like Moses whom the Lord saw face to face," it is understandable that tradition ascribed to Moses the sentence quoted and its whole sequel. But what is understandable or plausible is not as such certain. The narrator does not claim to have heard the account from God; perhaps he heard it from some man or men; perhaps he retells a tale. The Bible continues: "And the earth was unformed and void. . . . " It is not clear whether the earth thus described was created by God or antedated His creation. [But it is quite clear that while speaking about how the earth looked at first, the Bible is silent about how heaven looked at first. The earth, i.e., that which is not heaven, seems to be more important than heaven.] This impression is confirmed by the sequel.

God created everything in six days. On the first day He created light; on the second, heaven; on the third, the earth, the seas and vegetation; on the fourth, sun, moon and the stars; on the fifth, the water animals and the birds; and on the sixth, the land animals and man. The most striking difficulties are these: light and hence days (and nights) are presented as preceding the sun, and vegetation is presented as preceding the sun. The first difficulty is disposed of by the observation that creation-days are not sun-days. One must add however at once that there is a connection between the two kinds of days, for there is a connection, a correspondence between light and sun. The account of creation manifestly consists of two parts, the first part dealing with the first three creation-days and the second part dealing with the last three. The first part begins with the creation of light and the second with the creation of the heavenly light-givers. Correspondingly the first part ends with the creation of vegetation and the second with the creation of man. All creatures dealt with in the first part lack local motion; all creatures dealt with in the second part possess local motion. Vegetation precedes the sun because vegetation lacks local motion and the sun possesses it. Vegetation belongs to the earth; it is rooted in the earth; it is the fixed covering of the fixed earth. Vegetation was brought forth by the earth at God's command; the Bible does not speak of God's "making" vegetation; but as regards the living beings in question, God commanded the earth to bring them forth and yet God "made" them. Vegetation was created at the end of the first half of the creation-days; at the end of the last half the living beings that spend their whole lives on the firm earth were created. The living beings—beings that possess life in addition to local motion—were created on the fifth and sixth days, on the days following the day on which the heavenly light-givers were created. The Bible presents the creatures in an ascending order. Heaven is lower than earth. The heavenly light-givers lack life; they are lower than the lowliest living beast; they serve the living creatures, which are to be found only beneath heaven; they have been created in order to rule over day and night: they have not been made in order to rule over the earth, let alone over man. The most striking characteristic of the biblical account of creation is its demoting or degrading of heaven and the heavenly lights. Sun, moon and stars precede the living things because they are lifeless: they are not gods. What the heavenly lights lose, man gains; man is the peak of creation. The creatures of the first three days cannot change their places; the heavenly bodies change their places but not their courses; the living beings change their courses but not their "ways"; men alone can change their "ways." Man is the only being created in God's image. Only in the case of man's creation does the biblical account of creation repeatedly speak of God's "creating" him; in the case of the creation of heaven and the heavenly bodies that account speaks of God's "making" them. Only in the case of man's creation does the Bible intimate that there is a multiplicity in God: "Let us make man in our image, after our likeness. . . . So God created man in his image, in the image of God he created him; male and female he created them." Bisexuality is not a preserve of man; but only man's bisexuality could give rise to the view that there are gods and goddesses: there is no biblical word for "goddess." Hence creation is not begetting. The biblical account of creation teaches silently what the Bible teaches elsewhere explicitly but not therefore more emphatically: there is only one God, the God whose name is written as the Tetragrammaton, the living God who lives from ever to ever, who alone has created heaven and earth and all their hosts; He has not created any gods and hence there are no gods beside Him. The many gods whom men worship are either nothings that owe such being as they possess to man's making them, or if they are something (like sun, moon and stars), they surely are not gods. All nonpolemical references to "other gods" occurring in the Bible are fossils whose preservation indeed poses a question but only a rather unimportant one. Not only did the biblical God not create any gods; on the basis of the biblical account of creation one could doubt whether He created any beings one would be compelled to call "mythical": heaven and earth and all their hosts are always accessible to man as man. One would have to start from this fact in order to understand why the Bible contains so many sections that, on the basis of the distinction between mythical (or legendary) and historical, would have to be described as historical.

According to the Bible, creation was completed by the creation of man; creation culminated in the creation of man. Only after the creation of man did God "see all that he had made, and behold, it was very good." What then is the origin of the evil or the bad? The biblical answer seems to be that since everything of divine origin is good, evil is of human origin. Yet if God's creation as a whole is very good, it does not follow that all its parts are good or that creation as a whole contains no evil whatever: God did not find all parts of His creation to be good. Perhaps creation as a whole cannot be "very good" if it does not contain some evils. There cannot be light if there is not darkness, and the darkness is as much created as is light: God creates evil as well as He makes peace. However this may be, the evils whose origin the Bible lays bare after it has spoken of creation, are a particular kind of evils: the evils that beset man. Those evils are not due to creation or implicit in it, as the Bible shows by setting forth man's original condition. In order to set forth that condition, the Bible must retell man's creation by making man's creation as much as possible the sole theme. This second account answers the question, not of how heaven and earth and all their hosts have come into being but of how human life as we know it—beset with evils with which it was not beset originally—has come into being. This second account may only supplement the first account but it may also correct it and thus contradict it. After all, the Bible never teaches that one can speak about creation without contradicting oneself. In post-biblical parlance, the mysteries of the Torah (*sithre torah*) are the contradictions of the Torah; the mysteries of God are the contradictions regarding God.

The first account of creation ended with man; the second account begins with man. According to the first account God created man and only man in His image; according to the second account, God formed man from the dust of the earth and He blew into his nostrils the breath of life; the second account makes clear that man consists of two profoundly different ingredients, a high one and a low one. According to the first account it would seem that man and woman were created simultaneously; according to the second account man was created first. The life of man as we know it, the life of most men, is that of tillers of the soil; their life is needy and harsh; they need rain which is not always forthcoming when they need it and they must work hard. If human life had been needy and harsh from the very beginning, man would have been compelled or at least irresistibly tempted to be harsh, uncharitable, unjust; he would not have been fully responsible for his lack of charity or justice. But man is to be fully responsible. Hence the harshness of human life must be due to man's fault. His original condition must have been one of ease: he was not in need of rain nor of hard work; he was put by God into a well-watered garden that was rich in trees good for food. While man was created for a life of ease, he was not created for a life of luxury: there was no gold or precious stones in the garden of Eden. Man was created for a simple life. Accordingly, God permitted him to eat of every tree of the garden except of the tree of knowledge of good and evil (bad), "for in the day that you eat of it, you shall surely die." Man was not denied knowledge; without knowledge he could not have known the tree of knowledge nor the woman nor the brutes; nor could he have understood the prohibition. Man was denied knowledge of good and evil, i.e., the knowledge sufficient for guiding himself, his life. While not being a child he was to live in child-like simplicity and obedience to God. We are free to surmise that there is a connection between the demotion of heaven in the first account and the prohibition against eating of the tree of knowledge in the second. While man was forbidden to eat of the tree of knowledge, he was not forbidden to eat of the tree of life.

Man, lacking knowledge of good and evil, was content with his condition and in particular with his loneliness. But God, possessing knowledge of good and evil, found that "it is not good for man to be alone, so I will make him a helper as his counterpart." So God formed the brutes and brought them to man, but they proved not to be the desired helpers. Thereupon God formed the woman out of a rib of the man. The man welcomed her as bone of his bones and flesh of his flesh but, lacking knowledge of good and evil, he did not call her good. The narrator adds that "therefore [namely because the woman is bone of man's bone and flesh of his flesh] a man leaves his father and his mother, and cleaves to his wife, and they become one flesh." Both were naked but, lacking knowledge of good and evil, they were not ashamed.

Thus the stage was set for the fall of our first parents. The first move came from the serpent, the most cunning of all the beasts of the field; it seduced the woman into disobedience and then the woman seduced the man. The seduction moves from the lowest to the highest. The Bible does not tell what induced the serpent to seduce the woman into disobeying the divine prohibition against eating of the tree of knowledge of good and evil. It is reasonable to assume that the serpent acted as it did because it was cunning, i.e., possessed a low kind of wisdom, a congenital malice; everything that God has created would not be very good if it did not include something congenitally bent on mischief. The serpent begins its seduction by suggesting that God might have forbidden man and woman to eat of any tree in the garden, i.e., that God's prohibition might be malicious or impossible to comply with. The woman corrects the serpent and in so doing makes the prohibition more stringent than it was: "we may eat of the fruit of the other trees of the garden; it is only about the tree in the middle of the garden that God said: you shall not eat of it or touch it, lest you die." God did not forbid the man to touch the fruit of the tree of knowledge of good and evil. Besides, the woman does not explicitly speak of the tree of knowledge; she may have had in mind the tree of life. Moreover, God had said to the man: "thou mayest eat . . . thou wilt die"; the woman claims that God had spoken to both her and the man. She surely knew the divine prohibition only through human tradition. The serpent assures her that they will not die, "for God knows that when you eat of it, your eyes will be opened and you will be like God, knowing good and evil." The serpent tacitly questions God's veracity. At the same time it glosses over the fact that eating of the tree involves disobedience to God. In this it is followed by the woman. According to the serpent's assertion, knowledge of good and evil makes man immune to death, but we cannot know whether the serpent believes this. But could immunity to death be a great good for beings that did not know good and evil, to men who were like children? But the woman, having forgotten the divine prohibition, having therefore in a manner tasted of the tree of knowledge, is no longer wholly unaware of good and evil: she "saw that the tree was good for eating and a delight to the eyes and that the tree was to be desired to make one wise"; therefore she took of its fruit and ate. She thus made the fall of the man almost inevitable, for he was cleaving to her: she gave some of the fruit of the tree to the man, and he ate. The man drifts into disobedience by following the woman. After they had eaten of the tree, their eyes were opened and they knew that they were naked, and they sewed fig leaves together and made themselves aprons: through the fall they became ashamed of their nakedness; eating of the tree of knowledge of good and evil made them realize that nakedness is evil (bad).

The Bible says nothing to the effect that our first parents fell because they were prompted by the desire to be like God; they did not rebel high-handedly against God; they rather forgot to obey God; they drifted into disobedience. Nevertheless God punished them severely. He also punished the serpent. But the punishment did not do away with the fact that, as God Himself said, as a consequence of his disobedience "man has become like one of us, knowing good and evil." As a consequence there was now the danger that man might eat of the tree of life and live forever. Therefore God expelled him from the garden and made it impossible for him to return to it. One may wonder why man, while he was still in the garden of Eden, had not eaten of the tree of life of which he had not been forbidden to eat. Perhaps he did not think of it because, lacking knowledge of good and evil, he did not fear to die and, besides, the divine prohibition drew his attention away from the tree of life to the tree of knowledge.

The Bible intends to teach that man was meant to live in simplicity, without knowledge of good and evil. But the narrator seems to be aware of the fact that a being that can be forbidden to strive for knowledge of good and evil, i.e., that can understand to some degree that knowledge of good and evil is evil for it, necessarily possesses such knowledge. Human suffering from evil presupposes human knowledge of good and evil and vice versa. Man wishes to live without evil. The Bible tells us that he was given the opportunity to live without evil and that he cannot blame God for the evils from which he suffers. By giving man that opportunity God convinces him that his deepest wish cannot be fulfilled. The story of the fall is the first part of the story of God's education of man. This story partakes of the unfathomable character of God.

Man has to live with knowledge of good and evil and with the sufferings inflicted on him because of that knowledge or its acquisition. Human goodness or badness presupposes that knowledge and its concomitants. The Bible gives us the first inkling of human goodness and badness in the story of the first brothers. The oldest brother, Cain, was a tiller of the soil; the youngest brother, Abel, a keeper of sheep. God preferred the offering of the keeper of sheep who brought the choicest of the firstlings of his flock, to that of the tiller of the soil. This preference has more than one reason, but one reason seems to be that the pastoral life is closer to original simplicity than the life of the tillers of the soil. Cain was vexed and despite his having been warned by God against sinning in general, killed his brother. After a futile attempt to deny his guilt — an attempt that increased his guilt ("Am I my brother's keeper?") — he was cursed by God as the serpent and the soil had been after the Fall, in contradistinction to Adam and Eve who were not cursed; he was punished by God, but not with death: anyone slaying Cain would be punished much more severely than Cain himself. The relatively mild punishment of Cain cannot be explained by the fact that murder had not been expressly forbidden, for Cain possessed some knowledge of good and evil, and he knew that Abel was his brother, even assuming that he did not know that man was created in the image of God. It is better to explain Cain's punishment by assuming that punishments were milder in the beginning than later on. Cain — like his fellow fratricide Romulus — founded a city, and some of his descendants were the ancestors of men practicing various arts: the city and the arts, so alien to man's original simplicity, owe their origin to Cain and his race rather than to Seth, the substitute for Abel, and his race. It goes without saying that this is not the last word of the Bible on the city and the arts but it is its first word, just as the prohibition against eating of the tree of knowledge is, as one may say, its first word simply and the revelation of the Torah, i.e., the highest kind of knowledge of good and evil that is vouchsafed to men, is its last word. One is also tempted to think of the difference between the first word of the first book of Samuel on human kingship and its last word. The account of the race of Cain culminates in the song of Lamech who boasted to his wives of his slaying of men, of his being superior to God as an avenger. The (antediluvian) race of Seth cannot boast of a single inventor; its only distinguished members were Enoch who walked with God and Noah who was a righteous man and walked with God: civilization and piety are two very different things.

By the time of Noah the wickedness of man had become so great that God repented of His creation of man and all other earthly creatures, Noah alone excepted; so He brought on the Flood. Generally speaking, prior to the Flood man's life span was much longer than after it. Man's antediluvian longevity was a relic of his original condition. Man originally lived in the garden of Eden where he could have eaten of the tree of life and thus have become immortal. The longevity of antediluvian man reflects this lost chance. To this extent the transition from antediluvian to postdiluvian man is a decline. This impression is confirmed by the fact that before the Flood rather than after it the sons of God consorted with the daughters of man and thus generated the mighty men of old, the men of renown. On the other hand, the fall of our first parents made possible or necessary in due time God's revelation of His Torah, and this was decisively prepared, as we shall see, by the Flood. In this respect the transition from antediluvian to postdiluvian mankind is a progress. The ambiguity regarding the Fall—the fact that it was a sin and hence evitable and that it was inevitable—is reflected in the ambiguity regarding the status of antediluvian mankind.

The link between antediluvian mankind and the revelation of the Torah is supplied by the first Covenant between God and men, the Covenant following the Flood. The Flood was the proper punishment for the extreme and well-nigh universal wickedness of antediluvian men. Prior to the Flood mankind lived, so to speak, without restraint, without law. While our first parents were still in the garden of Eden, they were not forbidden anything except to eat of the tree of knowledge. The vegetarianism of antediluvian men was not due to an explicit prohibition (cf. Gen. 1:29); their abstention from meat belongs together with their abstention from wine (cf. Gen. 9:20); both were relics of man's original simplicity. After the expulsion from the garden of Eden, God did not punish men, apart from the relatively mild punishment which He inflicted on Cain. Nor did He establish human judges. God as it were experimented, for the instruction of mankind, with mankind living in freedom from law. This experiment just as the experiment with men remaining like innocent children, ended in failure. Fallen or awake man needs restraint, must live under law. But this law must not be simply imposed. It must form part of a Covenant in which God and man are equally, though not equal, partners. Such a partnership was established only after the Flood; it did not exist in antediluvian times either before or after the Fall. The inequality regarding the Covenant is shown especially by the fact that God's undertaking never again to destroy almost all life on earth as long as the earth lasts is not conditioned on all men or almost all men obeying the laws promulgated by God after the Flood: God's promise is made despite, or because of, His knowing that the devisings of man's heart are evil from his youth. Noah is the ancestor of all later men just as Adam was; the purgation of the earth through the Flood is to some extent a restoration of mankind to its original state; it is a kind of second creation. Within the limits indicated, the condition of postdiluvian men is superior to that of antediluvian men. One point requires special emphasis: in the legislation following the Flood, murder is expressly forbidden and made punishable with death on the ground that man was created in the image of God (Gen. 9:6). The first Covenant brought an increase in hope and at the same time an increase in punishment. Man's rule over the beasts, ordained or established from the beginning, was only after the Flood to be accompanied by the beasts' fear and dread of man (cf. Gen. 9:2 with Gen. 1:26–30 and 2:15).

The Covenant following the Flood prepares the Covenant with Abraham. The Bible singles out three events that took place between the Covenant after the Flood and God's calling Abraham: Noah's curse of Canaan, a son of Ham; the excellence of Nimrod, a grandson of Ham; and men's attempt to prevent their being scattered over the earth through building a city and a tower with its top in the heavens. Canaan whose land came to be the promised land, was cursed because of Ham's seeing the nakedness of his father Noah, because of Ham's transgressing a most sacred, if unpromulgated, law; the curse of Canaan was accompanied by the blessing of Shem and Japheth who turned their eyes away from the nakedness of their father; here we have the first and the most fundamental division of mankind, at any rate of postdiluvian mankind, the division into a cursed and a blessed part. Nimrod was the first to be a mighty man on earth—a mighty hunter before the Lord; his kingdom included Babel; big kingdoms are attempts to overcome by force the division of mankind; conquest and hunting are akin to one another. The city that men built in order to remain together and thus to make a name for themselves was Babel; God scattered them by confounding their speech, by bringing about the division of mankind into groups speaking different languages, groups that cannot understand one another: into nations, i.e., groups united not only by descent but by language as well. The division of mankind into nations may be described as a milder alternative to the Flood.

The three events that took place between God's Covenant with mankind after the Flood and His calling Abraham point to God's way of dealing with men knowing good and evil and devising evil from their youth; well-nigh universal wickedness will no longer be punished with well-nigh universal destruction; well-nigh universal wickedness will be prevented by the division of mankind into nations in the sense indicated; mankind will be divided, not into the cursed and the blessed (the curses and blessings were Noah's, not God's), but into a chosen nation and the nations that are not chosen. The emergence of nations made it possible that Noah's Ark floating alone on the waters covering the whole earth be replaced by a whole, numerous nation living in the midst of the nations covering the whole earth. The election of the holy nation begins with the election of Abraham. Noah was distinguished from his contemporaries by his righteousness; Abraham separates himself from his contemporaries and in particular from his country and kindred at God's command—a command accompanied by God's promise to make him a great nation. The Bible does not say that this primary election of Abraham was preceded by Abraham's right-eousness. However this may be, Abraham shows his righteousness by at once obeying God's command, by trusting in God's promise the fulfillment of which he could not possibly live to see, given the short lifespans of postdiluvian men: only after Abraham's offspring will have become a great nation, will the land of Canaan be given to them forever. The fulfillment of the promise required that Abraham not remain childless, and he was already quite old. Accordingly, God promised him that he would have issue. It was Abraham's trust in God's promise that, above everything else, made him righteous in the eyes of the Lord. It was God's intention that His promise be fulfilled through the offspring of Abraham and his wife Sarah. But this promise seemed to be laughable to Abraham, to say nothing of Sarah: Abraham was one hundred years old and Sarah ninety. Yet nothing is too wondrous for the Lord. The laughable announcement became a joyous announcement. The joyous announcement was followed immediately by God's announcement to Abraham of His concern with the wickedness of the people of Sodom and Gomorra. God did not yet know whether those people were as wicked as they were said to be. But they might be; they might deserve total destruction as much as the generation of the Flood. Noah had accepted the destruction of his generation without any questioning. Abraham, however, who had a deeper trust in God, in God's righteousness, and a deeper awareness of his being only dust and ashes than Noah, presumed in fear and trembling to appeal to God's righteousness lest He, the judge of the whole earth, destroy the righteous along with the wicked. In response to Abraham's insistent plead-ing, God as it were promised to Abraham that He would not destroy Sodom if ten righteous men were found in the city: He would save the city for the sake of the ten righteous men within it. Abraham acted as the mortal partner in God's righteousness; he acted as if he had some share in the responsibility for God's acting righteously. No wonder that God's Covenant with Abraham was incompar-ably more incisive than His Covenant immediately following the Flood.

Abraham's trust in God thus appears to be the trust that God in His righteousness will not do anything incompatible with His righteousness and that while or because nothing is too wondrous for the Lord, there are firm boundaries set to Him by His righteousness, by Him. This awareness is deepened and therewith modified by the last and severest test of Abraham's trust: God's command to him to sacrifice Isaac, his only son from Sarah. Before speaking of Isaac's conceptions and birth, the Bible speaks of the attempt made by Abimelech, the king of Gerar, to lie with Sarah; given Sarah's old age Abimelech's action might have forestalled the last opportunity that Sarah bear a child to Abraham; therefore God intervened to prevent Abimelech from approaching Sarah. A similar danger had threatened Sarah many years earlier at the hands of the Pharaoh; at that time she was very beautiful. At the time of the Abimelech incident she was apparently no longer very beautiful, but despite her being almost ninety years old she must have been still quite attractive; this could seem to detract from the wonder of Isaac's birth. On the other hand, God's special intervention against Abimelech enhances that wonder. Abraham's supreme test presupposes the wondrous character of Isaac's birth: the very son who was to be the sole link between Abraham and the chosen people and who was born against all reasonable expectations, was to be sacrificed by his father. This command contradicted, not only the divine promise, but also the divine prohibition against the shedding of innocent blood. Yet Abraham did not argue with God as he had done in the case of Sodom's destruction. In the case of Sodom, Abraham was not confronted with a divine command to do something and in particular not with a command to surrender to God, to render to God, what was dearest to him: Abraham did not argue with God for the preservation of Isaac because he loved God, and not himself or his most cherished hope, with all his heart, with all his soul and with all his might. The same concern with God's righteousness that had induced him to plead with God for the preservation of Sodom if ten just men should be found in that city, induced him not to plead for the preservation of Isaac, for God rightfully demands that He alone be loved unqualifiedly: God does not command that we love His chosen people with all our heart, with all our soul and with all our might. The fact that the command to sacrifice Isaac contradicted the prohibition against the shedding of innocent blood, must be understood in the light of the difference between human justice and divine justice: God alone is unqualifiedly, if unfathomably, just. God promised to Abraham that He would spare Sodom if ten righteous men should be found in it, and Abraham was satisfied with this promise; He did not promise that He would spare it if nine righteous men were found in it; would those nine be destroyed together with the wicked? And even if all Sodomites were wicked and hence justly destroyed, did their infants who were destroyed with them deserve their destruction? The apparent contradiction between the command to sacrifice Isaac and the divine promise to the descendants of Isaac is disposed of by the consideration that nothing is too wondrous for the Lord. Abraham's supreme trust in God, his simple, single-minded, childlike faith was rewarded, although or because it presupposed his entire unconcern with any reward, for Abraham was willing to forgo, to destroy, to kill the only reward with which he was concerned; God prevented the sacrifice of Isaac. Abraham's intended action needed a reward although he was not concerned with a reward because his intended action cannot be said to have been intrinsically rewarding. The preservation of Isaac is as wondrous as his birth. These two wonders illustrate more clearly than anything else the origin of the holy nation.

The God who created heaven and earth, who is the only God, whose only image is man, who forbade man to eat of the tree of knowledge of good and evil, who made a Covenant with mankind after the Flood and thereafter a Covenant with Abraham which became His Covenant with Abraham, Isaac and Jacob—what kind of God is He? Or, to speak more reverently and more adequately, what is His name? This question was addressed to God Himself by Moses when he was sent by Him to the sons of Israel. God replied: "Ehyeh-Asher-Ehyeh." This is mostly translated: "I am that (who) I am." One has called that reply "the metaphysics of Exodus" in order to indicate its fundamental character. It is indeed the fundamental biblical statement about the biblical God, but we hesitate to call it metaphysical, since the notion of *physis* is alien to the Bible. I believe that we ought to render this statement by "I shall be what I shall be," thus preserving the connection between God's name and the fact that He makes covenants with men, i.e., that He reveals Himself to men above all by His commandments and by His promises and His fulfillment of the promises. "I shall be what I shall be" is as it were explained in the verse (Exod. 33:19), "I shall be gracious to whom I shall be gracious and I shall show mercy to whom I shall show mercy." God's actions cannot be predicted, unless He Himself predicted them, i.e., promised them. But as is shown precisely by the account of Abraham's binding of Isaac, the way in which He fulfills His promises cannot be known in advance. The biblical God is a mysterious God: He comes in a thick cloud (Exod. 19:4); He cannot be seen; His presence can be sensed but not always and everywhere; what is known of Him is only what He chose to communicate by His word through His chosen servants. The rest of the chosen people know His word—apart from the Ten Commandments (Deut. 4:12 and 5:4–5)—only mediately and does not wish to know it immediately (Exod. 20:19 and 21, 24:1-2, Deut. 18:15-18, Amos 3:17). For almost all purposes the word of God as revealed to His prophets and especially to Moses became *the* source of knowledge of good and evil, the true tree of knowledge which is at the same time the tree of life.

This much about the beginning of the Bible and what it entails. Let us now cast a glance at some Greek counterparts to the beginning of the Bible and in the first place at Hesiod's *Theogony* as well as the remains of Parmenides' and Empedocles' works. They all are the works of known authors. This does not mean that they are, or present themselves as, merely human. Hesiod sings what the Muses, the daughters of Zeus who is the father of gods and men, taught him or commanded him to sing. One could say that the Muses vouch for the truth of Hesiod's song, were it not for the fact that they sometimes say lies resembling what is true. Parmenides transmits the teachings of a goddess, and so does Empedocles. Yet these men composed their books; their songs or speeches are books. The Bible on the other hand is not a book. The utmost one could say is that it is a collection of books. But are all parts of that collection books? Is in particular the Torah a book? Is it not rather the work of an unknown compiler or of unknown compilers who wove together writings and oral traditions of unknown origin? Is this not the reason why the Bible can contain fossils that are at variance even with its fundamental teaching regarding God? The author of a book in the strict sense excludes everything that is not necessary, that does not fulfill a function necessary for the purpose that his book is meant to fulfill. The compilers of the Bible as a whole and of the Torah in particular seem to have followed an entirely different rule. Confronted with a variety of preexisting holy speeches, which as such had to be treated with the utmost respect, they excluded only what could not by any stretch of the imagination be rendered compatible with the fundamental and authoritative teaching; their very piety, aroused and fostered by the preexisting holy speeches, led them to make such changes in those holy speeches as they did make. Their work may then abound in contradictions and repetitions that no one ever intended as such, whereas in a book in the strict sense there is nothing that is not intended by the author. Yet by excluding what could not by any stretch of the imagination be rendered compatible with the fundamental and authoritative teaching, they prepared the traditional way of reading the Bible, i.e., the reading of the Bible as if it were a book in the strict sense. The tendency to read the Bible and in particular the Torah as a book in the strict sense was infinitely strengthened by the belief that it is the only holy writing or the holy writing par excellence.

Hesiod's *Theogony* sings of the generation or begetting of the gods; the gods were not "made" by anybody. So far from being created by a god, earth and heaven are the ancestors of the immortal gods. More precisely, according to Hesiod everything that is has come to be. First there arose Chaos, Gaia (Earth) and Eros. Gaia gave birth first to Ouranos (Heaven) and then, mating with Ouranos, she brought forth Kronos and his brothers and sisters. Ouranos hated his children and did not wish them to come to light. At the wish and advice of Gaia, Kronos deprived his father of his generative power and thus unintentionally brought about the emergence of Aphrodite; Kronos became the king of the gods. Kronos's evil deed was avenged by his son Zeus whom he had generated by mating with Rheia and whom he had planned to destroy; Zeus dethroned his father and thus became the king of the gods, the father of gods and men, the mightiest of all the gods. Given his ancestors it is not surprising that while being the father of men and belonging to the gods who are the givers of good things, he is far from being kind to men. Mating with Mnemosyne, the daughter of Gaia and Ouranos, Zeus generated the nine Muses. The Muses give sweet and gentle eloquence and understanding to the kings whom they wish to honor. Through the Muses there are singers on earth, just as through Zeus there are kings. While kingship and song may go together, there is a profound difference between the two—a difference that, guided by Hesiod, one may compare to that between the hawk and the nightingale. Surely Metis (Wisdom), while being Zeus's first spouse and having become inseparable from him, is not identical with him; the relation of Zeus and Metis may remind one of the relation of God and Wisdom in the Bible. Hesiod speaks of the creation or making of men not in the *Theogony* but in his *Works and Days,* i.e., in the context of his teaching regarding how man should live, regarding man's right life, which includes the teaching regarding the right seasons (the "days"): the question of the right life does not arise regarding the gods. The right life for man is the just life, the life devoted to working, especially to tilling the soil. Work thus understood is a blessing ordained by Zeus who blesses the just and crushes the proud: often even a whole city is destroyed for the deeds of a single bad man. Yet Zeus takes cognizance of men's justice and injustice only if he so wills. Accordingly, work appears to be not a blessing but a curse: men must work because the gods keep hidden from them the means of life and they do this in order to punish them for Prometheus's theft, inspired by philanthropy, of fire. But was not Prometheus's action itself prompted by the fact that men were not properly provided for by the gods and in particular by Zeus? Be this as it may, Zeus did not deprive men of the fire that Prometheus had stolen for them; he punished them by sending Pandora to them with her box that was filled with countless evils such as hard toils. The evils with which human life is beset, cannot be traced to human sin. Hesiod conveys the same message by his story of the five races of men which came into being successively. The first race, the golden race, was made by the gods while Kronos was still ruling in heaven; these men lived without toil and grief; they had all good things in abundance because the earth by itself gave them abundant fruit. Yet the men made by father Zeus lack this bliss; Hesiod does not make clear whether this is due to Zeus's ill will or to his lack of power; he gives us no reason to think that it is due to man's sin. He creates the impression that human life became ever more miserable as one race of men succeeds the other: there is no divine promise, supported by the fulfillment of earlier divine promises, that permits one to trust and to hope.

The most striking difference between the poet Hesiod and the philosophers Parmenides and Empedocles is that according to the philosophers not everything has come into being: that which truly is, has not come into being and does not perish. This does not necessarily mean that what is always is a god or gods. For if Empedocles, e.g., calls one of the eternal four elements Zeus, this Zeus has hardly anything in common with what Hesiod, or the people generally, understood by Zeus. At any rate according to both philosophers the gods as ordinarily understood have come into being, just as heaven and earth, and therefore will perish again.

At the time when the opposition between Jerusalem and Athens reached the level of what one may call its classical struggle, in the twelfth and thirteenth centuries, philosophy was represented by Aristotle. The Aristotelian god like the biblical God is a thinking being, but in opposition to the biblical God he is only a thinking being, pure thought: pure thought that thinks itself and only itself. Only by thinking himself and nothing but himself does he rule the world. He surely does not rule by giving orders and laws. Hence he is not a creator-god: the world is as eternal as god. Man is not his image: man is much lower in rank than other parts of the world. For Aristotle it is almost a blasphemy to ascribe justice to his god; he is above justice as well as injustice.

It is often been said that the philosopher who comes closest to the Bible is Plato. This was said not the least during the classical struggle between Jerusalem and Athens in the Middle Ages. Both Platonic philosophy and biblical piety are animated by the concern with purity and purification: the "pure reason" in Plato's sense is closer to the Bible than the "pure reason" in Kant's sense or for that matter in Anaxagoras's and Aristotle's sense. Plato teaches, just as the Bible, that heaven and earth were created or made by an invisible God whom he calls the Father, who is always, who is good and hence whose creation is good. The coming-into-being and the preservation of the world that he has created depends on the will of its maker. What Plato himself calls the theology consists of two teachings: 1) God is good and hence is no way the cause of evil; 2) God is simple and hence unchangeable. On the divine concern with men's justice and injustice, the Platonic teaching is in fundamental agreement with the biblical teaching; it even culminates in a statement that agrees almost literally with biblical statements. Yet the differences between the Platonic and the biblical teaching are no less striking than the agreements. The Platonic teaching on creation does not claim to be more than a likely tale. The Platonic God is a creator also of gods, of visible living beings, i.e., of the stars; the created gods rather than the creator God create the mortal living beings and in particular man; heaven is a blessed god. The Platonic God does not create the world by his word; he creates it after having looked to the eternal ideas which therefore are higher than he. In accordance with this, Plato's explicit theology is presented within the context of the first discussion of education in the *Republic,* within the context of what one may call the discussion of elementary education; in the second and final discussion of education — the discussion of the education of the philosophers — theology is replaced by the doctrine of ideas. As for the thematic discussion of providence in the *Laws,* it may suffice here to say that it occurs within the context of the discussion of penal law.

In his likely tale of how God created the visible whole, Plato makes a distinction between two kinds of gods, the visible cosmic gods and the traditional gods — between the gods who revolve manifestly, i.e., who manifest themselves regularly, and the gods who manifest themselves so far as they will. The least one would have to say is that according to Plato the cosmic gods are of much higher rank than the traditional gods, the Greek gods. Inasmuch as the cosmic gods are accessible to man as man—to his observations and calculations—, whereas the Greek gods are accessible only to the Greeks through Greek traditions, one may ascribe in comic exaggeration the worship of the cosmic gods to the barbarians. This ascription is made in an altogether noncomic manner and intent in the Bible: Israel is forbidden to worship the sun and the moon and the stars which the Lord has allotted to the other peoples everywhere under heaven. This implies that the other peoples', the barbarians', worship of the cosmic gods is not due to a natural or rational cause, to the fact that those gods are accessible to man as man but to an act of God's will. It goes without saying that according to the Bible the God who manifests Himself as far as He wills, who is not universally worshipped as such, is the only true god. The Platonic statement taken in conjunction with the biblical statement brings out the fundamental opposition of Athens at its peak to Jerusalem: the opposition of the God or gods of the philosophers to the God of Abraham, Isaac and Jacob, the opposition of Reason and Revelation.

The Tree of Knowledge: Genesis 3

Martin Buber

The biblical account of the so-called fall of man (Genesis 3) may well be founded upon a primeval myth of the envy and vengeance of gods, of whose contents we have no more than an inkling: the story that has been written down and preserved for us has acquired a very different meaning. The divine being whose actions are here recorded is repeatedly referred to (with the exception of the dialogue between the serpent and the woman) by an appellation, alien to the style of the rest of the Bible, which is compounded out of a proper name—interpreted elsewhere (Exod. 3:14 f.) as He-is-there—and a generic term which is plural in form and corresponds most nearly to our "Godhead." This God is the sole possessor of the power both of creation and of destiny; He is surrounded by other celestial beings, but all these are subject to Him and without names or power of their own. Of course, He does not impose His will upon man, the last of His works; He does not compel him, He only commands, or rather forbids, him, albeit under a severe threat. The man—and with him his woman, who was not created till after the prohibition had been pronounced, but who appears to have become cognizant of it in some peculiar manner while still a rib within the body of the man—may give or withhold his obedience, for he is at liberty; they are both at liberty to accede to their creator or to refuse themselves to Him. Yet their transgression of the prohibition is not reported to us as a decision between good and evil, but as something other, of whose otherness we must take account.

The terms of the dialogue with the serpent are already strange enough. It speaks as though it knew very imprecisely what it obviously knows very precisely. "Indeed, God has said: You shall not eat of every tree of the garden . . . " it

---

From *On the Bible: Eighteen Studies by Martin Buber.* © 1968 by Schocken Books Inc.

says and breaks off. Now the woman talks, but she too intensifies God's prohibition and adds to it words He did not use: " . . . touch it not, else you must die." As becomes manifest subsequently, the serpent is both right and wrong in denying that this will be the consequence: they do not have to die after eating, they merely plunge into *human* mortality, that is, into the knowledge of death to come—the serpent plays with the word of God, just as Eve played with it. And now the incident itself begins: the woman regards the tree. She does not merely see that it is a delight to the eye, she also sees in it that which cannot be seen: how good its fruit tastes and that it bestows the gift of understanding. This seeing has been explained as a metaphorical expression for perceiving, but how could these qualities of the tree be perceived? It must be a contemplation that is meant, but it is a strange, dreamlike kind of contemplation. And so, sunk in contemplation, the woman plucks, eats, and hands to the man, and now he eats also, whose presence has till then been revealed to us by neither word nor gesture—she seems moved by dream-longing, but it seems to be truly in dream-lassitude that he takes and eats. The whole incident is spun out of play and dream; it is irony, a mysterious irony of the narrator, that spins it. It is apparent: the two doers know not what they do; more than this, they can only do it, they cannot know it. There is no room here for the pathos of the two principles, as we see it in the ancient Iranian religion, the pathos of the choice made by the Two themselves and by the whole of mankind after them.

And nevertheless both of them, good and evil, are to be found here—but in a strange, ironical shape, which the commentators have not understood as such and hence have not understood at all.

The tree of whose forbidden fruit the first humans eat is called the tree of the knowledge of good and evil; so does God Himself also call it. The serpent promises that by partaking of it, they would become like God, knowers of good and evil; and God seems to confirm this when He says subsequently that they have thereby become "as one of us," to know good and evil. This is the repetitive style of the Bible; the antitheses constantly reappear in fresh relationships with one another: its purpose is to demonstrate with superclarity that it is they we are dealing with. But nowhere is their meaning intimated. The words may denote the ethical antithesis, but they may also denote that of beneficial and injurious, or of delightful and repulsive; immediately after the serpent's speech the woman "sees" that the tree is "good to eat," and immediately upon God's prohibition followed His dictum that it was "not good" that man should be alone—the adjective translated by "evil" is equally indefinite.

In the main, throughout the ages, three interpretations have repeatedly emerged in explanation of what the first humans acquired by partaking of the fruit. One, which refers to the acquisition of sexual desire, is precluded both by the fact of the creation of man and woman as sexually mature beings and by the concept of "becoming like God," which is coupled with the "knowledge of good and evil": this God is suprasexual. The other interpretation, relating to the acquisition of moral consciousness, is no less contrary to the nature of this God: we have only to think of the declaration in His mouth that man, now that he has acquired moral consciousness, must not be allowed to attain aeonian life as well! According to the third interpretation, the meaning of this "knowledge of good and evil" is nothing else than: cognition in general, cognizance of the world, knowledge of all the good and bad things there are, for this would be in line with biblical usage, in which the antithesis good and evil is often used to denote "anything," "all kinds of things." But this interpretation, the favorite one today, is also unfounded. There is no place in the Scriptures where the antithesis meant simply "anything" or "all kinds of things"; if all those passages that are taken as having this significance are examined in relation to the concrete nature of the current situation and the current intention of the speaker, they are always found to refer in actual fact to an affirmation or a negation of both good and bad, of both favorable and unfavorable. The "be it . . . be it . . . ," which is always found in this context, does not relate to the whole scale of that which is, inclusive of everything neutral, but precisely to the opposites and to discrimination between them, even though knowing them is bound up with knowing "everything in the world." Thus it is stated, for instance, as of the angel as the heavenly, so of the king as the earthly representative of God, that he knows all things (2 Sam. 14:20); but where it is said of him that he discerns the good and the evil (2 Sam. 14:17), this refers specifically to the knowledge of the right and the wrong, the guilty and the innocent, which the earthly judge, like the heavenly who rules over the nations (cf. Pss. 82:2 and 58:2), receives from his divine commissioner, so that he may give it practical realization. But added to this is the fact that the word sequence "good and evil" (without an article) — which, apart from our tale, only occurs on one other occasion, in a subsequent passage that is dependent upon this one (Deut. 1:39) — is given an emphasis in the story of Paradise, by repetition and other stylistic means, that does not permit us to suppose it a rhetorical flourish. Neither is it the case that "cognition in general" only came to the first humans when they partook of the fruit: it is not before a creature without knowledge that, even before the creation of the woman, God brings the beasts that he may give them their appointed names, but before the bearer of His own breath, the being upon whom, at the very hour of creation, He had manifestly bestowed the abundance of knowledge contained in speech, of which that being is now the master.

"Knowledge of good and evil" means nothing else than: cognizance of the opposites that the early literature of mankind designated by these two terms;

they still include the fortune and the misfortune or the order and the disorder that are experienced by a person, as well as that which he causes. This is still the same in the early Avestic texts, and it is the same in those of the Bible which precede written prophecy and to which ours belongs. In the terminology of modern thought, we can transcribe what is meant as: adequate awareness of the opposites inherent in all being within the world. And that, from the viewpoint of the biblical creation-belief, means: adequate awareness of the opposites latent in creation.

We can only reach complete understanding if we remain fully aware that the basic conception of all the theo- and anthropology of the Hebrews, namely the immutable difference and distance that exist between God and man, irrespective of the primal fact of the latter's "likeness" to God and of the current fact of his "nearness" to Him (Ps. 73:28), also applies to the knowledge of good and evil. This knowledge as the primordial possession of God and the same knowledge as the magical attainment of man are worlds apart in their nature. God knows the opposites of being, which stem from His own act of creation; He encompasses them, untouched by them; He is as absolutely familiar with them as He is absolutely superior to them; He has direct intercourse with them (this is obviously the original meaning of the Hebrew verb "know": be in direct contact with), and this in their function as the opposite poles of the world's being. For as such He created them—we may impute this late biblical doctrine (Isa. 45:7) to our narrator, in its elementary form. Thus He who is above all opposites has intercourse with the opposites of good and evil that are of His own making; and something of His primordial familiarity with them He appears, as can be gathered from the words "one of us" (Gen. 3:22), to have bestowed upon the "sons of God" (Gen. 6:2) by virtue of their share in the work of creation. The "knowledge" acquired by man through eating the miraculous fruit is of an essentially different kind. A superior-familiar encompassing of opposites is denied to him who, despite his "likeness" to God, has a part only in that which is created and not in creation, is capable only of begetting and giving birth, not of creating. Good and evil, the yes-position and the no-position of existence, enter into his living cognizance; but in him they can never be temporally coexistent. He knows oppositeness only by his situation within it; and that means de facto (since the yes can present itself to the experience and perception of man in the no-position, but not the no in the yes-position): he knows it directly from within that "evil" at times when he happens to be situated there. More exactly: he knows it when he recognizes a condition in which he finds himself whenever he has transgressed the command of God, as the "evil" and the one he has thereby lost and which, for the time being, is inaccessible to him, as the good. But at this point, the process in the human soul becomes a process in the world: through the recognition of oppositeness, the opposites which are always latently present in creation break out into actual reality; they become existent.

In just this manner the first humans, as soon as they have eaten of the fruit, "know" that they are naked. "And the eyes of both of them were opened": they see themselves as they are, but now, since they see themselves so, not merely without clothing, but "naked." Recognition of this fact, the only recorded consequence of the magical partaking, cannot be adequately explained on the basis of sexuality, although without the latter it is, of course, inconceivable. Admittedly, they had not been ashamed before one another and now they are ashamed, not merely before one another, but with one another before God (Gen. 3:10), because, overcome by the knowledge of oppositeness, they feel the natural state of unclothedness in which they find themselves to be an ill or an evil, or rather both at once and more besides, and by this very feeling they make it so; but as a countermeasure they conceive, will, and establish the "good" of clothing. One is ashamed of being as one is because one now "recognizes" this so-being in its oppositional nature as an intended shall-be; but now it has really become a matter for shame. In themselves, naturally, neither the concept of clothed- and unclothedness, nor that of man and woman before one another, has anything whatsoever to do with good and evil; human "recognition" of opposites alone brings with it the fact of their relatedness to good and evil. In this lamentable effect of the great magic of the becoming like God the narrator's irony becomes apparent; an irony whose source was obviously great suffering through the nature of man.

But does not God Himself confirm that the serpent's promise has been fulfilled? He does; but this most extreme expression, this pronouncement, "Man is become as one of us, to know good and evil," is also still steeped in the ironic dialectic of the whole, which, it here shows most clearly, does not emanate from an intention freely formed by the narrator, but is imposed upon him by the theme—which corresponds exactly to his suffering through the nature of man—at this stage of its development. Because man is now numbered among those who know good and evil, God wishes to prevent him from also eating of the tree of life and "living forever." The narrator may have taken the motif from the ancient myth of the envy and vengeance of gods: if so, it acquired through him a meaning fundamentally different from its original one. Here there can no longer be any expression of fear that man might now become a match for the celestial beings: we have just seen how earthly is the nature of man's knowledge of "good and evil." The "like one of us" can be uttered here only in the ironic dialectic. But now it is the irony of a "divine compassion." God, who breathed His breath into the construction of dust, placed him in the garden of the four rivers and give him a helpmate, wanted him to accept His continued guidance; He wanted to protect him from the opposites latent in existence. But man—caught up in demonry, which the narrator symbolizes for us with his web of play and dream—withdrew at once from both the will of God and from His protection and, though without properly understanding what he was doing, nevertheless with this deed, unrealized by his understanding, caused the latent opposites to break out at the most dangerous point, that of the world's closest proximity to God. From that moment on, oppositeness takes hold of him, not indeed as a must-sin—of that, and hence of original sin, there is no question here—but as the ever-recrudescent reaction to the no-position and its irredeemable perspective; he will ever anew find himself naked and look around for fig leaves with which to plait himself a girdle. This situation would inevitably develop into full demonry, if no end were set to it. Lest the thoughtless creature, again without knowing what he is doing, long for the fruit of the other tree and eat himself into aeons of suffering, God prevents his return to the garden from which He expelled him in punishment. For man as a "living soul" (Gen. 2:7), known death is the threatening boundary; for him as the being driven round amid opposites, it may become a haven, the knowledge of which brings comfort.

This stern benefaction is preceded by the passing of sentence. It announces no radical alteration of that which already exists; it is only that all things are drawn into the atmosphere of oppositeness. When she gives birth, for which she was prepared at the time of her creation, woman shall suffer pains such as no other creature suffers—henceforth a price must be paid for being human; and the desire to become once more one body with the man (cf. Gen. 2:24) shall render her dependent upon him. To the man work, which was already planned for him before he was set in the garden, shall become an affliction. But the curse conceals a blessing. From the *seat,* which had been made ready for him, man is sent out upon a *path,* his own, the human path. That this is the path into the world's history, that only through it does the world have a history—and a historical goal—must, in his own way, have been felt by the narrator.

Composite Artistry: P and J

Robert Alter

A technique of placing two parallel accounts in dynamically complementary sequence is splendidly evident at the very beginning of the Hebrew Bible. There are, of course, two different creation stories. The first, generally attributed to P, begins with Genesis 1:1 and concludes with the report of the primeval sabbath (Gen. 2:1–3), probably followed, as most scholars now think, by a formal summary in the first half of Gen. 2:4: "Such is the story of heaven and earth when they were created." The second version of the creation story, taken from the J Document, would then begin with the subordinate clause in the second half of Gen. 2:4, "When the Lord God made earth and heaven . . . ," going on to the creation of man, the vegetable world, the animal kingdom, and woman, in that order, and after the completion of creation proper at the end of Chapter 2, moving directly into the story of the serpent and the banishment from Eden.

Now, it is obvious enough that the two accounts are complementary rather than overlapping, each giving a different *kind* of information about how the world came into being. The P writer (for convenience, I shall refer to him in the singular even if this source may have been the product of a "school") is concerned with the cosmic plan of creation and so begins appropriately with the primordial abyss whose surface is rippled by a wind from (or spirit of) God. The J writer is interested in man as a cultivator of his environment and as a moral agent, and so he begins with a comment on the original lack of vegetation and irrigation and ends with an elaborate report of the creation of woman. There are also, however, certain seeming contradictions between the two versions. According to P, the sequence

From *The Art of Biblical Narrative.* © 1981 by Robert Alter. Basic Books, 1981. Originally entitled "Composite Artistry."

of creation is vegetation, animal life, and finally humanity. Although the chronology of acts of creation is not so schematically clear in J, the sequence there, as we have already noted, would appear to be man, vegetation, animal life, woman. In any case, the most glaring contradiction between the two versions is the separation of the creation of woman from the creation of man in J's account. P states simply, "Male and female He created them," suggesting that the two sexes came into the world simultaneously and equally. J, on the other hand, imagines woman as a kind of divine afterthought, made to fill a need of man, and made, besides, out of one of man's spare parts.

Why should the author of Genesis have felt obliged to use both these accounts, and why did he not at least modify his sources enough to harmonize the contradictions? The scholars—who of course refer to him as redactor, not author—generally explain that he viewed his inherited literary materials as canonical, which meant both that he had to incorporate them and that he could not alter them. What of early Hebrew writings may have seemed canonical in, say, the fifth century B.C.E., or what that may have meant at the time is a matter of pure conjecture; but the text we have of the creation story has a coherence as significant form which we can examine, and I would argue that there were compelling literary reasons for the Genesis author to take advantage of both documents at his disposal—perhaps also rejecting others about which we do not know—and to take advantage as well of the contradictions between his sources. These reasons should become apparent through some close attention to the stylistic and thematic differences between the two creation stories.

Although P begins, according to the general convention of opening formulas for ancient Near Eastern creation epics, with an introductory adverbial clause, "When God began to create heaven and earth," his prose is grandly paratactic, moving forward in a stately parade of parallel clauses linked by "and" (the particle vav). Or, to switch the metaphor of motion, the language and the represented details of P's account are all beautifully choreographed. Everything is numerically ordered; creation proceeds through a rhythmic process of incremental repetition; each day begins with God's world-making utterance ("And God said . . . ") and ends with the formal refrain, "It was evening and it was morning," preceded in five instances by still another refrain, "And God saw that it was good." P's narrative emphasizes both orderly sequence and a kind of vertical perspective, from God above all things down to the world He is creating. God is the constant subject of verbs of generation and the source of lengthy creative commands reported as direct speech. (By contrast, in J's version, there is a whole block of verses [Gen. 2:10–14] where God is entirely absent as subject; man, moreover, performs independent action and utters speech; and the only direct discourse in the whole chapter assigned to God is His command to Adam not to eat from the Tree of Knowledge and His brief statement about man's need for a helpmate.)

The orderliness of P's vision is expressed in another kind of symmetry that is both stylistic and conceptual: creation, as he represents it, advances through a series of balanced pairings, which in most instances are binary oppositions. J also begins by mentioning the creation of earth and heaven (significantly, earth comes first for him), but he makes nothing of the opposition in the development of his story, while P actually builds his picture of creation by showing how God splits off the realm of earth from the realm of heaven, sets luminaries in the heavens to shine on the earth, creates the birds of the heavens above together with the swarming things of the seas below. Darkness and light, night and day, evening and morning, water and sky, water and dry land, sun and moon, grass and trees, bird and sea-creature, beast of the field and creeping thing of the earth, human male and female — each moment of creation is conceived as a balancing of opposites or a bifurcation producing difference in some particular category of existence. In the first half of chapter 1 (verses 1–19), for the first four days of creation, before the appearance of animate creatures, the governing verb, after the reiterated verbs of God's speaking, is "to divide," suggesting that the writer was quite aware of defining creation as a series of bifurcations or splittings-off. God divides primordial light from primordial darkness, the upper waters from the lower, day from night, terrestrial light from terrestrial darkness. In the second half of the story, as we pass on to the creation of the animal realm, the verbs of division disappear, and with the fuller details pertaining to animals and man, the symmetry is a little looser, less formulaic. Nevertheless, bracketed pairs continue. to inform the account of cosmogony, and there is also a noticeable tendency to recapitulate many of the previous terms of creation as the narrative proceeds. The conclusion in the first sabbath vividly illustrates the emphatic stylistic balance, the fondness for parallelisms and incremental repetitions that mark P's entire account (Gen. 2:2–3):

> And God completed on the seventh day His work which He had made.
> And he ceased on the seventh day from all His work which He had made.
> And God blessed the seventh day and He hallowed it.
> For on it He had ceased from all His work which God created to make.

We have here not only incremental repetition but, as I have tried to show through this rather literal translation, a tightly symmetrical envelope structure, the end returning to the beginning: the first line of the passage ends with God's making or doing, as does the last, while the end of the last line, by also introducing the seemingly redundant phrase "God created," takes us all the way back to the opening of the creation story, "When God began to create." In P's magisterial formulation, everything is ordered, set in its appointed place, and contained within a symmetrical frame.

All this reflects, of course, not simply a bundle of stylistic predilections but a particular vision of God, man, and the world. Coherence is the keynote of creation. Things come into being in orderly progression, measured in a numerical sequence which is defined by the sacred number seven. Law, manifested in the symmetrical dividings that are the process of creation and in the divine speech that initiates each stage of creation, is the underlying characteristic of the world as God makes it. Man, entering the picture climactically just before it is declared complete on the seventh day, is assigned a clearly demarcated role of dominance in a grand hierarchy. In this version of cosmogony, God, as Einstein was to put it in his own argument against randomness, decidedly does not play dice with the universe, though from a moral or historical point of view that is exactly what He does in J's story by creating man and woman with their dangerous freedom of choice while imposing upon them the responsibility of a solemn prohibition.

J's strikingly different sense of the movement of creation makes itself felt from the outset in his syntax and in the rhythms of his prose. Instead of stylistic balance and stately progression, he begins with a subordinate clause that leads us into a long and sinuous complex sentence which winds its way through details of landscape and meteorology to the making of man (Gen. 2:4b–7):

> At the time when the Lord God was making earth and heaven, no shrub of the field yet being on the earth and no grain of the field yet having sprouted, for the Lord God had not made rain fall on the earth and there was no man to work the soil, but a flow would well up from the earth to water the whole surface of the soil — then the Lord God fashioned man from clods of the soil and blew into his nostrils the breath of life, and man became a living being.

J needs this kind of ramified syntax, so unlike P's, because he constantly sees his subject in a complex network of relations that are causal, temporal, mechanical, and, later in the chapter, moral and psychological as well. His prose imparts a sense of rapid and perhaps precarious forward movement very different from P's measured parade from first day to seventh. It is a movement of restless human interaction with the environment, even in Eden: here man *works* the soil, which cannot realize its full inventory of nourishing plant life until that work has begun; in P's version, man, more grandly and more generally, has dominion over the natural world. Man as J imagines him is more essentially bound to the natural world, formed out of a humble clod, his name, *'adam,* in a significant etymological pun, derived from *'adamah,* soil. He is one with the earth as he is not in P's hierarchical sequence; but he is also apart from it by virtue of the very faculty of consciousness that enables him to give things their names, and by virtue of the free will through which he will cause himself to be banished from the Garden, henceforth to work the soil as an arduous punishment rather than as a natural function.

P is interested in the large plan of creation; J is more interested in the complicated and difficult facts of human life in civilization, for which he provides an initial explanation through the story of what happened in Eden. Man culminates the scheme of creation in P, but man is the narrative center of J's story, which is quite another matter. P's verbs for creation are "to make" (*'asoh*) and "to create" (*baro'*), while J has God "fashioning" (*yatzor*), a word that is used for potters and craftsmen, and also makes him the subject of concrete agricultural verbs, planting and watering and causing to grow.

J's concern with the mechanics of things is continuous with his vision of God, man, and history. The world is stuff to be worked and shaped through effort, for both man and God; language has its role in ordering things, but it is not, as in P, generative. If man's role as worker of the earth is stressed at both the beginning and the end of the Eden story, one might also infer that God's work with man does not cease with the fashioning into creaturehood of the original clod of earth. In this version of creation, there is moral tension between man and God—a notion not hinted at in P—and also, as God's solicitude for man's loneliness shows, there is divine concern for man. It is instructive that here no speech of God occurs until He addresses man and reflects on man's condition. The verb "to say," which in the first account of creation introduced each of the divine utterances through which the world was brought into being, here is used to designate *thought* or interior speech, the brief divine monologue in which God ponders man's solitude and resolves to alleviate it (Gen. 2:18): "And the Lord God said, 'It is not good for man to be alone. I shall make him an aid fit for him.' "

The differences between our two versions are so pronounced that by now some readers may be inclined to conclude that what I have proposed as a complementary relationship is in fact a contradictory one. If, however, we can escape the modern provincialism of assuming that ancient writers must be simple because they are ancient, it may be possible to see that the Genesis author chose to combine these two versions of creation precisely because he understood that his subject was essentially contradictory, essentially resistant to consistent linear formulation, and that this was his way of giving it the most adequate literary expression. Let me explain this first in the notorious contradiction about the creation of woman, and then go on to comment briefly on the larger cosmogonic issues.

It may make no logical sense to have Eve created after Adam and inferior to him when we have already been told that she was created at the same time and in the same manner as he, but it makes perfect sense as an account of the contradictory facts of woman's role in the post-Edenic scheme of things. On the one hand, the writer is a member of a patriarchal society in which women have more limited legal privileges and institutional functions than do men, and where social convention clearly invites one to see woman as subsidiary to man, her proper place, in the Psalmist's words, as a "fruitful vine in the corner of your house." Given such social facts and such entrenched attitudes, the story of Eve being made from an unneeded rib of Adam is a proper account of origins. On the other hand, our writer — one does not readily think of him as a bachelor — surely had a fund of personal observation to draw on which could lead him to conclude that woman, contrary to institutional definitions, could be a daunting adversary or worthy partner, quite man's equal in a moral or psychological perspective, capable of exerting just as much power as he through her intelligent resourcefulness. If this seems a fanciful inference, one need only recall the resounding evidence of subsequent biblical narrative, which includes a remarkable gallery of women — Rebekah, Tamar, Deborah, Ruth — who are not content with a vegetative existence in the corner of the house but, when thwarted by the male world or when they find it lacking in moral insight or practical initiative, do not hesitate to take their destiny, or the nation's, into their own hands. In the light of this extra-institutional awareness of woman's standing, the proper account of origins is a simultaneous creation of both sexes, in which man and woman are different aspects of the same divine image. "In the image of God He created him. Male and female He created them" (Gen. 1:27). The decision to place in sequence two ostensibly contradictory accounts of the same event is an approximate narrative equivalent to the technique of post-Cubist painting which gives us, for example, juxtaposed or superimposed, a profile and a frontal perspective of the same face. The ordinary eye could never see these two at once, but it is the painter's prerogative to represent them as a simultaneous perception within the visual frame of his painting, whether merely to explore the formal relations between the two views or to provide an encompassing representation of his subject. Analogously, the Hebrew writer takes advantage of the composite nature of his art to give us a tension of views that will govern most of the biblical stories — first, woman as man's equal sharer in dominion, standing exactly in the same relation to God as he; then, woman as man's subservient helpmate, whose weakness and blandishments will bring such woe into the world.

A similar encompassing of divergent perspectives is achieved through the combined versions in the broader vision of creation, man, and God. God is both transcendent and immanent (to invoke a much later theological opposition), both magisterial in His omnipotence and actively, empathically involved with His creation. The world is orderly, coherent, beautifully patterned, and at the same time it is a shifting tangle of resources and topography, both a mainstay and a baffling challenge to man. Humankind is the divinely appointed master of creation, and an internally divided rebel against the divine scheme, destined to scrabble a painful living from the soil that has been blighted because of man. The creation story might have been more "consistent" had it begun with Genesis 2:4b, but it would have lost much of its complexity as a satisfying account of a bewilderingly complex reality that involves the elusive interaction of God, man, and the natural world. It is of course possible, as scholars have tended to assume, that this complexity is the purely accidental result of some editor's pious compulsion to include disparate sources, but that is at least an ungenerous assumption and, to my mind, an implausible one as well.

The Struggle with the Angel:
Textual Analysis of Genesis 32:22–32

Roland Barthes

(22) And he rose up that night, and took his two wives, and his two women servants, and his eleven sons, and passed over the ford Jabbok. (23) And he took them, and sent them over the brook, and sent over that he had. (24) And Jacob was left alone; and there wrestled a man with him until the breaking of the day. (25) And when he saw that he prevailed not against him, he touched the hollow of his thigh; and the hollow of Jacob's thigh was out of joint as he wrestled with him. (26) And he said, Let me go, for the day breaketh. And he said, I will not let thee go, exept thou bless me. (27) And he said unto him, What is thy name? And he said, Jacob. (28) And he said, Thy name shall be called no more Jacob, but Israel: for as a prince hast thou power with God and with men, and hast prevailed. (29) And Jacob asked him, and said, Tell me, I pray thee, thy name. And he said, Wherefore is it thou dost ask after my name? And he blessed him there. (30) And Jacob called the name of the place Peniel: for I have seen God face to face, and my life is preserved. (31) And as he passed over Penuel the sun rose upon him, and he halted upon his thigh. (32) Therefore the children of Israel eat not of the sinew which shrank, which is upon the hollow of the thigh, unto this day: because he touched the hollow of Jacob's thigh in the sinew that shrank.

The clarifications — or precautionary remarks — which will serve as an introduction

From *Image, Music, Text.* © 1977 by Roland Barthes. English translation © 1977 by Stephen Heath. Hill and Wang, 1977.

to the following analysis will in fact be largely negative. First of all, it must be said that I shall not be giving any preliminary exposition of the principles, perspectives and problems of the structural analysis of narrative. That analysis is not a science nor even a discipline (it is not taught), but, as part of the newly developing semiology, it nevertheless represents an area of research which is becoming well known, so much so that to set out its prolegomena on the occasion of every fresh analysis would be to run the risk of producing an impression of useless repetition. Moreover, the structural analysis presented here will not be very pure. I shall indeed be referring in the main to the principles shared by all those semiologists concerned with narrative and, to finish, I shall even show how the piece under discussion lends itself to an extremely classic and almost canonical structural analysis, this orthodox consideration (orthodox from the point of view of the structural analysis of narrative) is all the more justified in that we shall be dealing with a mythical narrative that may have entered writing (entered Scripture) via an oral tradition. At the same time, however, I shall allow myself every so often (and perhaps continuously on the quiet) to direct my investigations towards an analysis with which I am more at home, textual analysis ("textual" is used with reference to the contemporary theory of the *text,* this being understood as production of *signifiance* and not as philological object, custodian of the Letter). Such an analysis endeavours to "see" each particular text in its difference—which does not mean in its ineffable individuality, for this difference is "woven" in familiar codes; it conceives the text as taken up in an *open* network which is the very infinity of language, itself structured without closure; it tries to say no longer *from where* the text comes (historical criticism), nor even *how* it is made (structural analysis), but how it is unmade, how it explodes, disseminates—by what coded paths it *goes off.* Finally, the last of these precautionary remarks and intended to forestall any disappointment, there is no question in what follows of a methodological confrontation between structural or textual analysis and exegesis, this lying outside my competence. I shall simply analyse the text of Genesis 32 (traditionally called "Jacob's struggle with the angel") as though I were at the first stage of a piece of research (which is indeed the case). What is given here is not a "result" nor even a "method" (which would be too ambitious and would imply a "scientific" view of the text that I do not hold), but merely a "way of proceeding."

I. SEQUENTIAL ANALYSIS

Structural analysis embraces roughly three types or three objects of analysis, or again, if one prefers, comprises three tasks. 1) The inventorization and classification of the "psychological," biographical, characterial and social attributes of the characters involved in the narrative (age, sex, external qualities, social situation or position of importance, etc.). Structurally, this is the area of indices (notations, of infinitely varied expression, serving to transmit a signified — as, for example, "irritability," "grace," "strength" — which the analyst names in his metalanguage; it being understood that the metalinguistic term may very well not figure directly in the text — as indeed is generally the case — which will not employ "irritability" or "grace" or whatever. If one establishes a homology between narrative and (the linguistic) sentence, then the indice corresponds to the adjective, to the *epithet* (which, let us not forget, was a figure of rhetoric). This is what we might call *indicial analysis*. 2) The inventorization and classification of the *functions* of the characters; what they do according to their narrative status, in their capacity as subject of an action that remains constant: the Sender, the Seeker, the Emissary, etc. In terms of the sentence, this would be the equivalent of the *present participle* and is that *actantial analysis* of which A. J. Greimas was the first to provide the theory. 3) The inventorization and classification of the *actions*, the plane of the *verbs*. These narrative actions are organized in sequences, in successions apparently ordered according to a pseudo-logical schema (it is a matter of a purely empirical, cultural logic, a product of experience — even if ancestral — and not of reasoning). What we have here is thus *sequential analysis*.

Our text lends itself, if in fact briefly, to indicial analysis. The contest it describes can be read as an indice of Jacob's strength (attested in other episodes of the chronicle of this hero's exploits) and that indice leads towards an anagogical meaning which is the (invincible) strength of God's Elect. Actantial analysis is also possible, but as the text is essentially made up of seemingly contingent actions it is better to work mainly on a sequential (or actional) analysis of the episode, being prepared in conclusion to add one or two remarks concerning the actantial. I shall divide the text (without, I think, forcing things) into three sequences: 1) the Crossing, 2) the Struggle, 3) the Namings.

1. *The Crossing* (Gen. 32:22–24). Let us straightaway give the schema of the sequences of this episode, a schema which is twofold or at least, as it were, "strabismic" (what is at stake here will be seen in a moment):

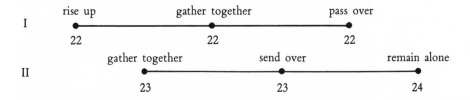

It can be noted at once that structurally *rise up* is a simple *operator for beginning;* one might say, putting things quickly, that by *rise up* is to be understood not only that Jacob starts moving but also that the discourse *gets underway*. The beginning of a narrative, of a discourse, of a text, is an extremely sensitive point — *where to begin?* The *said* must be torn from the *not-said*, whence a whole rhetoric of beginning *markers*. The most important thing, however, is that the two sequences (or sub-sequences) seem to be in a state of redundancy (which is perhaps usual in the discourse of the period: a piece of information is given and then repeated; but the rule here is reading, not the historical and philological determination of the text: we are reading the text not in its "truth" but in its "production" — which is not its "determination"). Paradoxically moreover (for redundancy habitually serves to homogenize, to clarify and assure a message), when read after two millennia of Aristotelian rationalism (Aristotle being the principal theoretician of classic narrative) the redundancy of the two sub-sequences creates an abrasion, a grating of readability. The sequential schema, that is, can be read in two ways: 1) Jacob himself crosses over the ford — if need be after having made several trips back and forth — and thus the combat takes place on the left bank of the flood (he is coming from the North) *after he has definitively crossed over;* in this case, *send over* is read *cross over himself;* 2) Jacob sends over but does not himself cross over; he fights on the right bank of the Jabbok *before crossing over,* in a rearguard position. Let us not look for some *true* interpretation (perhaps our very hesitation will appear ridiculous in the eyes of the exegetes); rather, let us consume two different pressures of readability: 1) if Jacob remains alone *before* crossing the Jabbok, we are led towards a "folkloric" reading of the episode, the mythical reference then being overwhelming which has it that a trial of strength (as for example with a dragon or the guardian spirit of a river) must be imposed on the hero *before* he clears the obstacle, *so that* — once victorious — he can clear it; 2) if on the contrary Jacob having crossed over (he and his tribe), he remains alone on the good side of the flood (the side of the country to which he wants to go), then the passage is without structural finality while acquiring on the other hand a religious finality: if Jacob is alone, it is no longer to settle the question of and obtain the crossing but in order that he be *marked* with solitude (the familiar *setting apart* of the one chosen by God). There is a historical circumstance which increases the undecidability of the two interpretations. Jacob's purpose is to return home, to enter the land of Canaan: given this, the crossing of the River Jordan would be easier to understand than that of the Jabbok. In short, we are confronted with the crossing of a spot that is neutral. The crossing is crucial if Jacob has to win it over the guardian of the place, indifferent if what is important is the solitude, the mark of Jacob. Perhaps we have here the tangled trace of two stories, or at least of two narrative instances: the one, more "archaic" (in the simple stylistic sense of the term), makes of the crossing itself an ordeal; the other, more "realist," gives a "geographical" air to Jacob's journey by mentioning the places he goes through (without attaching any mythical value to them).

If one carries back onto this twofold sequence the pattern of subsequent events, that is the Struggle and the Naming, the dual reading continues, coherent to the end in each of its two versions. Here again is the diagram:

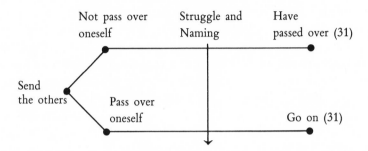

If the Struggle stands between the "not pass over" and the "have passed over" (the folklorizing, mythical reading), then the mutation of the Names corresponds to the very purpose of every etymological saga; if on the contrary the Struggle is only a stage between a position of immobility (of meditation, of election) and a movement of setting off again, then the mutation of the Name has the value of a spiritual rebirth (of "baptism"). All of which can be summarized by saying that in this first episode there is sequential readability but cultural ambiguity. No doubt the theologian would grieve at this indecision while the exegete would acknowledge it, hoping for some element of fact or argument that would enable him to put an end to it. The textual analyst, judging by my own impression, savours such *friction* between two intelligibilities.

2. *The Struggle* (Gen. 32:24–29). For the second episode we have once again to start from a complication (which is not to say a doubt) of readability—remember that textual analysis is founded on *reading* rather than on the objective structure of the text, the latter being more the province of structural analysis. This complication stems from the interchangeable character of the pronouns which refer to the two opponents in the combat: a style which a purist would describe as *muddled* but whose lack of sharpness doubtless posed no problem for Hebrew syntax. Who is "a man"? Staying within verse 25, is it "a man" who does not succeed in getting the better of Jacob or Jacob who cannot prevail over this someone? Is the "he" of "he prevailed not against him" (25) the same as the "he" of "And he said" (26)? Assuredly everything becomes clear in the end but it requires in some sort a retroactive reasoning of a syllogistic kind: you have vanquished God. He who is speaking to you is he whom you vanquished.

Therefore he who is speaking to you is God. The identification of the opponents is oblique, the readability is *diverted* (whence occasionally commentaries which border on total misunderstanding; as for example: "He wrestles with the Angel of the Lord and, thrown to the ground, obtains from him the certainty that God is with him").

Structurally, this amphibology, even if subsequently clarified, is not without significance. It is not in my opinion (which is, I repeat, that of a reader today) a simple complication of expression due to an unpolished, archaizing style; it is bound up with a paradoxical structure of the contest (paradoxical when compared with the stereotypes of mythical combat). So as to appreciate this paradox in its structural subtlety, let us imagine for a moment an endoxical (and no longer paradoxical) reading of the episode: A wrestles with B but fails to get the better of him; to gain victory at all costs, A then resorts to some exceptional strategy, whether an unfair and forbidden blow (the forearm chop in wrestling matches) or a blow which, while remaining within the rules, supposes a secret knowledge, a "dodge" (the "ploy" of the Jarnac blow [In 1547 Guy de Jarnac won a duel by an unexpected thrust which hamstrung his opponent]). *In the very logic of the narrative* such a blow, generally described as "decisive," brings victory to the person who administers it: the emphatic mark of which this blow is structurally the object cannot be reconciled with its being ineffective—by the very god of narrative it *must* succeed. Here, however, the opposite occurs: the decisive blow fails; A, who gave the blow, is not the victor; which is the structural paradox. The sequence then takes an unexpected course:

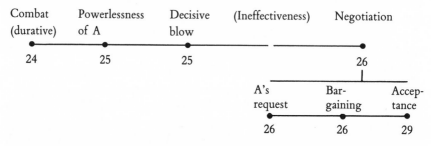

It will be noted that A (it matters little from the point of view of the structure if this be *someone, a man, God* or *the Angel*) is not strictly speaking vanquished but *held in check*. For this to be seen as a defeat, the adjunction of a *time limit* is needed: this is the breaking of day ("for the day breaketh" [26]), a notation which picks up verse 24 ("until the breaking of day") but now in the explicit context of a mythical structure. The theme of the nocturnal combat is structurally justified by the fact that at a certain moment, fixed in advance (as is the rising of the sun, as is the duration of a boxing match), the rules of the combat will no longer obtain, the structural play will come to an end, as too the supernatural play (the "demons" withdraw at dawn). Thus we can see that it is within a quite "regular" combat that the sequence sets up an unexpected readability, a logical surprise: the person who has the knowledge, the secret, the special ploy, is nevertheless defeated. The sequence itself, however actional, however anecdotal it may be, functions to *unbalance* the opponents in the combat, not only by the unforeseen victory of the one over the other, but above all (let us be fully aware of the *formal* subtlety of this surprise) by the illogical, *inverted*, nature of the victory. In other words (and here we find an eminently structural term, well known to linguists), the combat, as it is reversed in its unexpected development, *marks* one of the combatants: the weakest defeats the strongest, *in exchange for which* he is marked (on the thigh).

It is plausible (moving somewhat away from pure structural analysis and approaching textual analysis, vision *without barriers* of meanings) to fill out this schema of the mark (of the disequilibrium) with contents of an ethnological kind. The structural meaning of the episode, once again, is the following: a situation of balance (the combat at its outset) — and such a situation is a prerequisite for any marking (ascesis in Ignatius of Loyola for instance functions to establish the *indifference* of the will which allows the manifestation of the divine mark, the choice, the election) — is disturbed by the unlikely victory of one of the participants: there is an inversion of the mark, a counter-mark. Let us turn then to the family configuration. Traditionally, the line of brothers is in principle evenly balanced (they are all situated on the same level in relation to the parents); this equality of birth is normally unbalanced by the right of primogeniture: the eldest is marked. Now in the story of Jacob, there is an inversion of the mark, a counter-mark: it is the younger who supplants the elder (Gen. 27:36), taking his brother by the heel in order to reverse time; it is Jacob, the younger brother, who marks himself. Since Jacob has just obtained a mark in his struggle with God, one can say in a sense that A (God) is the substitute of the elder brother, once again beaten by the younger. The conflict with Esau is *displaced* (every symbol is a *displacement*; if the "struggle with the angel" is symbolic, then it has displaced something). Commentary — for which I am insufficiently equipped — would at this point doubtless have to widen the interpretation of the *inversion of the mark*, by placing it either in a historic-economic context — Esau is the eponym of the Edomites and there were economic ties between the Edomites and the Israelites; figured here perhaps is an overthrow of the alliance, the start of a new league of interests? — or in the field of the symbolic (in the psychoanalytical sense of the term) — the Old Testament seems to be less the world of the Fathers than that of the Enemy Brothers, the elder are ousted in favour of the younger; in the myth of the Enemy Brothers Freud pointed to the theme of *the smallest difference:*

is not the blow on the thigh, on the thin sinew, just such a *smallest difference?* Be that as it may, in this world God marks the young, acts against nature: his (structural) function is to constitute a *counter-marker.*

To conclude discussion of this extremely rich episode of the Struggle, of the Mark, I should like to add a remark as semiologist. We have seen that in the binary opposition of the combatants, which is perhaps the binary opposition of the Brothers, the younger is marked both by the reversal of the anticipated distribution of strengths and by a bodily sign, the touch on the thigh, the halting (not without recalling Oedipus, Swollen Foot, the Lame One). A mark is creative of meaning. In the phonological representation of language, the "equality" of the paradigm is unbalanced in favour of a marked element by the presence of a trait absent from its correlative and oppositional term. By marking Jacob (Israel), God (or the Narrative) permits an anagogical development of meaning, creates the formal operational conditions of a new "language," the election of Israel being its "message." God is a logothete, a founder of a language, and Jacob is here a "morpheme" of the new language.

3. *The Namings or Mutations* (Gen. 32:27–32). The object of the final sequence is the exchange of names, that is to say the promotion of new statuses, new powers. Naming is clearly related to Blessing: to bless (to accept the homage of a kneeling suppliant) and to name are both suzerain acts. There are two namings:

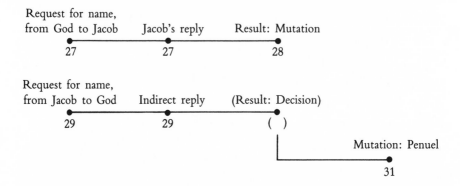

The mutation bears on Names, but in fact it is the entire episode which functions as *the creation of a multiple trace* — across Jacob's body, the status of the Brothers, Jacob's name of the place, the kind of food (creation of an alimentary taboo: the whole story can also be interpreted *a minimo* as the mythical foundation of a taboo). The three sequences that have been analysed are homological; what is in question in each is a *change* — of place, parental line, name, alimentary rite; all this keeping very close to an activity of language, a transgression of the rules of meaning.

Such is the sequential (or actional) analysis of our text. As has been seen, I have tried to remain always on the level of the structure, that is to say of the systematic correlation of the terms denoting an action. If I have chanced to mention certain possible meanings, the purpose has not been to discuss the probability of those meanings but rather to show how the structure "disseminates" contents—which each reading can make its own. My object is not the philological or historical document, custodian of a truth to be discovered, but the volume, the *signifiance* of the text.

II. STRUCTURAL ANALYSIS

The structural analysis of narrative being in part already constituted (by Propp, Lévi-Strauss, Greimas, Bremond), I wish to conclude—putting myself even more in the background—by confronting the text under discussion with two modes of structural analysis so as to demonstrate the interest of these two modes, though my own work has a somewhat different orientation: Greimas's actantial analysis and Propp's functional analysis.

1. *Actantial analysis.* The actantial grid worked out by Greimas [See especially A. J. Greimas, *Sémantique structurale* and *Du Sens*]—to be used, as he himself says, with prudence and flexibility—divides the characters, the actors, of a narrative into six formal classes of actants, defined by what they do according to narrative status and not by what they are psychologically (thus one actant may combine several characters just as a single character may combine several actants; an actant may also be figured by an inanimate entity). The "struggle with the angel" forms a very familiar episode in mythical narratives: the overcoming of an obstacle, the Ordeal. As far as the particular episode is concerned (things might perhaps be different over the whole set of Jacob's exploits), the actants are "filled" as follows: Jacob is the *Subject* (subject of the demand, the quest, the action); the *Object* (of the same demand, quest, action) is the crossing of the guarded and forbidden place, the flood, the Jabbok; the *Sender*, who sets in circulation the stake of the quest (namely the crossing of the flood), is obviously God; the *Receiver* is Jacob again (two actants are here present in a single figure); the *Opponent* (the one or ones who hinder the Subject in his quest) is God himself (it is he who, mythically, guards the crossing); the *Helper* (the one or ones who aid the Subject) is Jacob who provides help to himself through his own, legendary, strength (an indicial trait, as was noted).

The paradox, or at very least the anomic nature of the formulation, can be seen at once: that the subject be confounded with the receiver is banal; that the subject be his or her own helper is less usual (it generally occurs in "voluntarist" narratives or novels); but that the sender be the opponent is very rare and there is only one type of narrative that can present this paradoxical form—narratives relating an act of blackmail. If the opponent were only the (provisional) holder of the stake, then of course there would be nothing extraordinary: it is the opponent's role to have and defend ownership of the object that the hero wants to obtain (as with the dragon guarding a place to be crossed). Here however, as in every blackmail, God, at the same time that he guards the flood, also dispenses the mark, the privilege. The actantial form of the text is thus far from conciliatory: structurally, it is extremely audacious—which squares well with the "scandal" represented by God's defeat.

2. *Functional analysis.* Propp was the first to establish the structure of the folktale, by dividing it into its *functions* or narrative acts. [V. Propp, *Morphology of the Folktale.* Unfortunately, the word "function" is always ambiguous; at the beginning of the present piece we used it to define actantial analysis which assesses characters by their roles in the action (precisely their "function"); in Propp's terminology, there is a shift from character to the action itself, grasped in its *relations* to the actions surrounding it.] The functions, according to Propp, are stable elements, limited in number (some thirty or so) and always identical in their concatenation, even if occasionally certain functions are absent from this or that narrative. It so happens—as will be seen in a moment—that our text fulfills perfectly a section of the functional schema brought to light by Propp who would have been unable to imagine a more convincing application of his discovery.

In a preparatory section of the folktale (as analysed by Propp) there necessarily occurs an absence of the hero, something already the case in the tale of Jacob: Isaac sends Jacob far from his homeland to Laban (Gen. 28:2, 5). Our episode effectively begins at the fifteenth of Propp's narrative functions and can be coded in the following manner, showing at each stage the striking parallelism between Propp's schema and the Genesis narrative:

Propp and the folktale	*Genesis*
15. Transference from one place to another (by bird, horse, ship, etc.)	Set out from the North, from the Aramaeans, from the house of Laban, Jacob journeys home, to his father's house (29:1, Jacob sets out)
16. Combat between the Villain and the Hero	This is the sequence of the Struggle (32:24–27)
17. The hero is branded, "marked" (generally it is a matter of a mark on the body, but in other cases it is simply the gift of a jewel, of a ring)	Jacob is marked on the thigh (32:25–32)

18. Victory of the Hero, defeat of the Villain	Jacob's victory (32:26)
19. Liquidation of the misfortune or lack: the misfortune or lack had been established in the initial absence of the Hero: this absence is repaired	Having succeeded in crossing Penuel (32:31), Jacob reaches Schechem in Canaan (33:18)

There are other parallels. In Propp's function fourteen, the hero acquires the use of a magical object; for Jacob this talisman is obviously the blessing that he surprises his blind father into giving him (Genesis 27). Again, function twenty-nine represents the transfiguration of the hero (for example, the Beast transformed into a handsome nobleman); such a transfiguration seems to be present in the changing of the Name (Gen. 32:28) and the rebirth it implies. The narrative model stamps God with the role of the Villain (his *structural* role—it is not a question of a psychological role); the fact is that a veritable folktale stereotype can be read in the Genesis episode—the difficult crossing of a ford guarded by a hostile spirit. A further similitude between episode and tale is that in both cases character motivations (their reasons for acting) go unnoted, the ellipsis of such notations being not a stylistic element but a pertinent structural characteristic of the narration. Structural analysis in the strict sense of the term would thus conclude emphatically that the "struggle with the angel" is a true fairytale, since according to Propp all fairytales belong to the same structure, the one he described.

So we can see that what might be called the structural exploitation of the episode is very possible and even imperative. Let me indicate in conclusion, however, that what interests me most in this famous passage is not the "folkloristic" model but the abrasive frictions, the breaks, the discontinuities of readability, the juxtaposition of narrative entities which to some extent run free from an explicit logical articulation. One is dealing here (this at least is for me the savour of the reading) with a sort of *metonymic montage:* the themes (Crossing, Struggle, Naming, Alimentary Rite) are *combined,* not "developed." This abruptness, this asyndetic character of the narrative is well expressed by Hos. 12:3–4:

> "He took his brother by the heel in the womb / / and by his strength
> he had power with God."

Metonymic logic is that of the unconscious. Hence it is perhaps in that direction that one would need to pursue the present study, to pursue the reading of the text—its dissemination, not its truth. Evidently, there is a risk in so doing of weakening the episode's economic-historical force (certainly existent, at the level of the exchanges of tribes and the questions of power). Yet equally in so doing the symbolic explosion of the text (not necessarily of a religious order) is reinforced. The problem, the problem at least posed for me, is exactly to manage not to reduce the Text to a signified, whatever it may be (historical, economic, folkloristic or kerygmatic), but to hold its *signifiance* fully open.

Wrestling Sigmund: Three Paradigms for Poetic Originality

Harold Bloom

I begin with a parable, rather than a paradigm, but then I scarcely can distinguish between the two. The parable is Bacon's, and I have brooded on it before, as part of a meditation upon the perpetual (shall we say obsessive?) belatedness of strong poetry:

> The children of time do take after the nature and malice of the father. For as he devoureth his children, so one of them seeketh to devour and suppress the other, while antiquity envieth there should be new additions, and novelty cannot be content to add but it must deface.

I doubt that I have been able to add much to that dark observation of Bacon's, but I want again to swerve from it towards my own purposes. I don't read the ghastly image of malicious time devouring us as irony or allegory, but rather as sublime hyperbole, because of the terrible strength of the verb, "devouring." Time is an unreluctant Ugolino, and poems, as I read them, primarily are deliberate lies against that devouring. Strong poems reluctantly know, not Freud's parodistic Primal History Scene (*Totem and Taboo*) but what I have called the Scene of Instruction. Such a scene, itself both parable and paradigm, I have shied away from developing, until now, probably because of my own sense of trespass, my own guilt at having become a Jewish Gnostic after and in spite of an Orthodox upbringing. But without developing such a notion, I cannot go further, and so I must begin with it here.

We all choose our own theorists for the Scene of Instruction, or rather, as Coleridge would have said, we do not find their texts, but are found by

From *The Breaking of the Vessels.* © 1982 by The University of Chicago. The University of Chicago Press, 1982.

them. More often than not, these days, the theorists that advanced sensibilities are found by are the German language fourfold of Marx, Nietzsche, Freud, and Heidegger, but the inevitable precursor for formulating a Scene of Instruction has to be Kierkegaard, allied to Marx and Heidegger, involuntarily, by his antithetical relationship to Hegel. It may be that any Scene of Instruction has to be, rather like Derrida's Scene of Writing, more an unwilling parody of Hegel's quest than of Freud's. But I am content with a misprision of Kierkegaard, while being uneasily aware that his "repetition" is a trope that owes more than he could bear to the Hegelian trope of "mediation."

To talk about paradigms, however parabolically, in the context of poetry and criticism, is to engage the discourse of "repetition," in Kierkegaard's rather than Freud's sense of that term. I haven't ever encountered a useful discursive summary of Kierkegaard's notion, and I myself won't try to provide one, because Kierkegaard's idea of repetition is more trope than concept, and tends to defeat discursiveness. His little book *Repetition* is subtitled "An Essay in Experimental Psychology," but "experimental" is the crucial and tricky term, and modifies "psychology" into an odd blend of psychopoetics and theology. Repetition, we are told first, "is recollected forwards" and is "the daily bread which satisfies with benediction." Later, the book's narrator assures us that "repetition is always a transcendence," and indeed is "too transcendent" for the narrator to grasp. The same narrator, Constantine Constantius, wrote a long open letter against a Hegelian misunderstanding of his work, which insisted that true or anxious freedom willed repetition: "it is the task of freedom to see constantly a new side of repetition." Each new side is a "breaking forth," a "transition" or "becoming," and therefore a concept of happening, and not of being. If repetition, in this sense, is always a transition or a crossing, then the power of repetition lies in what its great American theorist, Emerson, called the shooting of a gap or the darting to an aim. Kierkegaard, unlike Emerson, was a Christian, and so his repetition cannot be only a series of transitions; eternity becomes true repetition.

But if we are more interested in poetry than in eternity, we can accept a limited or transitional repetition. We can say, still following the aesthetic stage in Kierkegaard, that Wallace Stevens *is* the repetition of Walt Whitman, or that John Ashbery *is* the repetition of Stevens. In this sense, repetition means the re-creation or revision of a paradigm, but of what paradigm? When a strong poet revises a precursor, he re-enacts a scene that is at once a catastrophe, a romance, and a transference. All three paradigms technically are tainted, though favorably from the perspective of poetry. The catastrophe is also a creation; the romance is incestuous; the transference violates taboo and its ambivalences. Are these three categories or one? What kind of a relational or dialectical event is at once creatively catastrophic, incestuously romantic, and ambivalently a metaphor for a trespass that *works?*

For an instance, I go back to the example of Wallace Stevens, still the poet of our moment. When I was a youngster, the academy view of Stevens was that of a kind of hothouse exquisite, vaguely perfumed, Ronald Firbank grown fat, and transmogrified into a Pennsylvania Dutchman practising insurance in Hartford, Connecticut. Now, in 1981, this vision has its own archaic charm, but thirty years ago it filled me with a young enthusiast's fury. I remember still the incredulous indulgence displayed by one of the masters of Yale New Criticism, now heartbreakingly mourned by me, when I read an essay in his graduate seminar suggesting that the seer of Hartford was the true ephebe of Walt Whitman, one of the roughs, an American. Stevens himself, a few miles up the road then, would have denied his own poetic father, but that after all is the most ancient of stories. I cite here again a small poem by the sane and sacred Walt that even Stevens confesses he had pondered deeply. The poem is called "A Clear Midnight":

> This is thy hour O Soul, thy free flight into the wordless,
> Away from books, away from art, the day erased, the lesson done,
> Thee fully forth emerging, silent, gazing, pondering the themes thou
>   lovest best,
> Night, sleep, death and the stars.

The Whitmanian soul, I take it, is the Coleridgean moon, the Arab of *Notes toward a Supreme Fiction.* Perhaps the ocean would have been redundant had it been lined up with night, sleep, and death, instead of "the stars," since moon and the tides are so intimately allied in the most pervasive of feminine tropes. We don't need the ocean anyway, since the moon as mother of the months is always the mother proper, Whitman's and our "fierce old mother," moaning for us to return whence we came. The mother's face is the purpose of the poem, as Keats told us implicitly, and Stevens in so many words. But the purpose of the poem, for the poet *qua* person, is Kenneth Burke's purpose, and not my own. The poet *qua* poet is my obsessive concern, and the Scene of Instruction creates the poet as or in a poet.

The Scene of Instruction in Stevens is a very belated phenomenon, and even Whitman's origins, despite all his mystifications, are shadowed by too large an American foreground. A better test for my paradigms is provided by the indubitable beginning of a canonical tradition. The major ancient possibilities are the Yahwist, the strongest writer in the Bible, and Homer. Beside them we can place Freud, whose agon with the whole of anteriority is the largest and most intense of our century. Because Freud has far more in common with the Yahwist than with Homer, I will confine myself here to the two Jewish writers, ancient and modern.

I want to interpret two difficult and haunting texts, each remarkable in several ways, but particularly as a startling manifestation of originality. One goes back to perhaps the tenth century before the Common Era; the other is nearly three thousand years later, and comes in our own time. The first is the story of Wrestling Jacob, and tells how Jacob achieved the name Israel, in Genesis 32:23–32, the author being that anonymous great writer, fully the equal of Homer, whom scholars have agreed to call by the rather Kafkan name of the letter J, or the Yahwist. The second I would call, with loving respect, the story of Wrestling Sigmund, and tells how Freud achieved a theory of the origins of the human sexual drive. As author we necessarily have the only possible modern rival of the Yahwist, Freud himself, the text being mostly the second of the *Three Essays on the Theory of Sexuality*.

Here is the text of Jacob's encounter with a daemonic being, as rendered literally by E. A. Speiser in the Anchor Bible:

> In the course of that night he got up and, taking his two wives, the two maidservants, and his eleven children, he crossed the ford of the Jabbok. After he had taken them across the stream, he sent over all his possessions. Jacob was left alone. Then some man wrestled with him until the break of dawn. When he saw that he could not prevail over Jacob, he struck his hip at its socket, so that the hip socket was wrenched as they wrestled. Then he said, "Let me go, for it is daybreak." Jacob replied, "I will not let you go unless you bless me." Said the other, "What is your name?" He answered, "Jacob." Said he, "You shall no longer be spoken of as Jacob, but as Israel, for you have striven with beings divine and human, and have prevailed." Then Jacob asked, "Please tell me your name." He replied, "You must not ask my name." With that, he bade him good-by there and then.
>
> Jacob named the site Peniel, meaning, "I have seen God face to face, yet my life has been preserved." The sun rose upon him just as he passed Penuel, limping on his hip.

I shall enhance my reputation for lunatic juxtapositions by citing next to this Sublime passage a cento of grotesque passages from Freud, the first two being from the second *Essay*, "Infantile Sexuality," and the third from *Essay* III, but summarizing the argument of the second *Essay:*

> It was the child's first and most vital activity, his sucking at his mother's breast, or at substitutes for it, that must have familiarized

him with this pleasure. The child's lips, in our view, behave like an *erotogenic zone*, and no doubt stimulation by the warm flow of milk is the cause of the pleasurable sensation. The satisfaction of the erotogenic zone is associated, in the first instance, with the satisfaction of the need for nourishment. To begin with, sexual activity props itself upon functions serving the purpose of self-preservation and does not become independent of them until later. No one who has seen a baby sinking back satiated from the breast and falling asleep with flushed cheeks and a blissful smile can escape the reflection that this picture persists as a prototype of the expression of sexual satisfaction in later life. The need for repeating the sexual satisfaction now becomes detached from the need for taking nourishment.

Our study of thumb-sucking or sensual sucking has already given us the three essential characteristics of an infantile sexual manifestation. At its origin it props itself upon one of the vital somatic functions; it has as yet no sexual object, and is thus *auto-erotic;* and its sexual aim is dominated by an *erotogenic zone.*

At a time at which the first beginnings of sexual satisfaction are still linked with the taking of nourishment, the sexual instinct has a sexual object outside the infant's own body in the shape of his mother's breast. It is only later that he loses it, just at the time, perhaps, when he is able to form a total idea of the person to whom the organ that is giving him satisfaction belongs. As a rule the sexual drive then becomes auto-erotic, and not until the period of latency has been passed through is the original relation restored. There are thus good reasons why a child sucking at his mother's breast has become the prototype of every relation of love. The finding of an object is in fact a re-finding of it.

Wrestling with a divine being or angel is rather a contrast to sucking at one's mother's breast, and achieving the name Israel is pretty well unrelated to the inauguration of the sexual drive. All that the Yahwist's and Freud's breakthroughs have in common is that they *are* breakthroughs, difficult to assimilate because these curious stories are each so *original.* But before I explore that common difficulty, I need to give a commentary upon each of these passages. What is the nature of Jacob's agon, and what does it mean to see Freud's own agon as being central to his theory of sexual origins?

To consider the Yahwist as being something other than a religious writer would be as eccentric as to consider Freud a religious writer despite himself.

But who sets the circumferences? All the academies, from the Academy of Ezra through the Academies of Alexandria on down to our own institutions, have in common their necessity for consensus. The Yahwist may have written to persuade, but he remains hugely idiosyncratic when compared either to the Elohist, who probably came a century after him, or to the much later Priestly Author, who may have belonged to the age of Ezra and the Return from Babylon, some six centuries after the Yahwist. E and P are far more normative than J, and far less original, in every meaning of "original." But I want to specify a particular aspect of J's originality, and it is one that I have never seen discussed as such. We are familiar, since the work of Nietzsche and of Burckhardt, with the ancient Greek concept of the agonistic, but we scarcely recognize an ancient Hebrew notion of agon, which is crucial throughout J's writing. J is an *unheimlich* writer, and perhaps the greatest master of the literary Sublime in what has become Western tradition. But J is also the most remarkable instance of what Blake meant, when in *The Marriage of Heaven and Hell* he characterized the history of all religions as choosing forms of worship from poetic tales. J's poetic tales of Yahweh and the Patriarchs are now so much the staple of Judaism and Christianity, and have been such for so long, that we simply cannot read them. Yet they were and are so original that there is quite another sense in which they never have been read, and perhaps cannot be read. If we allowed them their strangeness, then their uncanniness would reveal that tradition never has been able to assimilate their originality.

Yahweh appears to Abraham by the terebinths of Mamre; Abraham sits at the entrance of his tent as the day grows hot. He looks up, sees three men, one of them Yahweh, whom he recognizes, and invites them for an immediate meal. Yahweh and his angels devour rolls, curd, milk, and roast calf, while Abraham stands nearby. Yahweh then prophesies that Sarah, well past a woman's periods, will have a son. Sarah, listening behind Yahweh's back, at the tent entrance, laughs to herself. Yahweh, offended, asks rhetorically if anything is too much for him. Poor, frightened Sarah says she didn't laugh, but Yahweh answers: "Yes, you did."

What can we do with a Yahweh who sits on the ground, devours calf, is offended by an old woman's sensible derision, and then walks on to Sodom after being argued down by Abraham to a promise that he will spare that wicked city if he finds just ten righteous among the inhabitants? The silliest thing we can do is to say that J has an anthropomorphic concept of god. J doesn't have a concept of Yahweh; indeed we scarcely can say that J even has a conceptual image of Yahweh. J is nothing of a theologian, and everything of a storyteller, and his strong interest is personality, particularly the personality of Jacob. J's interest in Yahweh is intense, but rather less than J's concern for Jacob, because

Jacob is cannier and more agonistic even than Yahweh. Yahweh just about *is* the uncanny for J; what counts about Yahweh is that he is the source of the Blessing, and the Blessing is the aim of the agon, in total distinction from the Greek notion of agon.

The contest among the Greeks was for the foremost place, whether in chariot racing, poetry, or civic eminence. The subtle and superb Jacob knows only one foremost place, the inheritance of Abraham and of Isaac, so that tradition will be compelled to speak of the God of Abraham, the God of Isaac, the God of Jacob, the God of Judah. The Blessing means that the nation shall be known as Israel, the name that Jacob wins as agonist, and that the people shall be known as Jews after Judah, rather than say as Reubens, if that first-born had been chosen. Such a blessing achieves a pure temporality, and so the agon for it is wholly temporal in nature, whereas the Greek agon is essentially spatial, a struggle for the foremost place, and so for place, and not a mastery over time. That, I take it, is why temporality is at the center of the nightlong wrestling between Jacob and some nameless one among the Elohim, and I am now ready to describe that most significant of J's visions of agon.

I quote again Speiser's literal version of J's text:

> In the course of that night he got up and, taking his two wives, the two maidservants, and his eleven children, he crossed the ford of the Jabbok. After he had taken them across the stream, he sent over all his possessions. Jacob was left alone. Then some man wrestled with him until the break of dawn. When he saw that he could not prevail over Jacob, he struck his hip at its socket, so that the hip socket was wrenched as they wrestled. Then he said, "Let me go, for it is daybreak." Jacob replied, "I will not let you go unless you bless me." Said the other, "What is your name?" He answered, "Jacob." Said he, "You shall no longer be spoken of as Jacob, but as Israel, for you have striven with beings divine and human, and have prevailed." Then Jacob asked, "Please tell me your name." He replied, "You must not ask my name." With that, he bade him good-by there and then.
>
> Jacob named the site Peniel, meaning, "I have seen God face to face, yet my life has been preserved." The sun rose upon him just as he passed Penuel, limping on his hip.

So great is the uncanniness of this that we ought to approach J with a series of questions, rather than rely upon any traditional or even modern scholarly commentary whatsoever. Jacob has left Laban, and is journeying home, uneasily expecting a confrontation with his defrauded brother Esau. On the night before this dreaded reunion, Jacob supervises the crossing, into the land of the Blessing, of his household and goods. But then evidently he crosses back over the Jabbok so as to remain alone at Penuel in Transjordan. Why? J does not tell us, and instead suddenly confronts Jacob and the reader with "some man" who wrestles with Jacob until the break of dawn. About this encounter, there is nothing that is other than totally surprising. J's Jacob has been an agonist literally from his days in Rebecca's womb, but his last physical contest took place in that womb, when he struggled vainly with his twin Esau as to which should emerge first, Esau winning, but dragging out his tenacious brother, whose hand held on to his heel. Popular etymology interpreted the name Jacob as meaning "heel." Craft and wiliness have been Jacob's salient characteristics, rather than the physical strength evidently displayed in this nocturnal encounter. Yet that strength is tropological, and substitutes for the spiritual quality of persistence or endurance that marks Jacob or Israel.

Who is that "man," later called one of the Elohim, who wrestles with Jacob until dawn? And why should they wrestle anyway? Nothing in any tradition supports my surmise that this daemonic being is the Angel of Death, yet such I take him to be. What Jacob rightly fears is that he will be slain by the vengeful Esau on the very next day. Something after all is curiously negative and even fearful about Jacob's opponent. Rabbinical tradition explains this strange being's fear of the dawn as being an angel's pious fear lest he be late on Yahweh's business, but here as so often the Rabbis were weak misreaders of J. Everything about the text shows that the divine being's dread of daybreak is comparable to Count Dracula's, and only the Angel of Death is a likely candidate among the Elohim for needing to move on before sunrise. This wrestling match is not a ballet, but is deadly serious for both contestants. The angel lames Jacob permanently, yet even this cannot subdue the patriarch. Only the blessing, the new naming Israel, which literally means "May God persevere," causes Jacob to let go even as daylight comes. Having prevailed against Esau, Laban, and even perhaps against the messenger of death, Jacob deserves the agonistic blessing. In his own renaming of the site as Peniel, or the divine face, Jacob gives a particular meaning to his triumphal declaration that: "I have seen one of the Elohim face to face, and yet my life has been preserved." Seeing Yahweh face to face was no threat to Abraham's life, in J's view, but it is not Yahweh whom Jacob has wrestled to at least a standstill. I think there is no better signature of J's sublimity than the great sentence that ends the episode, with its powerful implicit contrast between Israel and the fled angel. Here is Jacob's true epiphany: "The sun rose upon him just as he passed Penuel, limping on his hip."

If there is an aesthetic originality in our Western tradition beyond interpretive assimilation, then it inheres in J's texts. We do not know Homer's precursors any more than we know J's, yet somehow we can see Homer as a revisionist, whereas J seems more unique. Is this only because Homer has been misread even more strongly than J has? The prophet Hosea is our first certain interpreter of Wrestling Jacob, and Hosea was a strong poet, by any standards, yet his text is not adequate to the encounter he describes. But Hosea's Yahweh was a rather more remote entity than J's, and Hosea did not invest himself as personally in Jacob as J seems to have done. What interpretive paradigm can help us read Jacob's contest strongly enough to be worthy of the uncanniness of J, an author who might be said impossibly to combine the antithetical strengths of a Tolstoy and a Kafka?

I recur to the distinction between the Hebrew temporal Sublime agon and the Greek spatial striving for the foremost place. Nietzsche, in his notes for the unwritten "untimely meditation" he would have called *We Philologists*, caught better even than Burckhardt the darker aspects of the Greek agonistic spirit:

> The agonistic element is also the danger in every development; it overstimulates the creative impulse. . . .
>
> The greatest fact remains always the precociously panhellenic HOMER. All good things derive from him; yet at the same time he remained the mightiest obstacle of all. He made everyone else superficial, and that is why the really serious spirits struggled against him. But to no avail. Homer always won.
>
> The destructive element in great spiritual forces is also visible here. But what a difference between Homer and the Bible as such a force!
>
> The delight in drunkenness, delight in cunning, in revenge, in envy, in slander, in obscenity — in everything which was *recognized* by the Greeks as human and therefore built into the structure of society and custom. The wisdom of their institutions lies in the lack of any gulf between good and evil, black and white. Nature, as it reveals itself, is not denied but only *ordered,* limited to specified days and religious cults. This is the root of all spiritual freedom in the ancient world; the ancients sought a moderate release of natural forces, not their destruction and denial.
>
> [TRANSLATED BY WILLIAM ARROWSMITH]

Whatever Nietzsche means by "the Bible" in that contrast to Homer, he is not talking accurately about J, the Bible's strongest writer. Not that J, with his obsessive, more-than-Miltonic sense of temporality, essentially agrees with Homer upon what constitutes spiritual freedom; no, perhaps J is further from Homer in that regard than even Nietzsche states. J does not discourse in good and evil, but in blessedness and unblessedness. J's subject, like Homer's, is strife, including the strife of gods and men. And drunkenness, delight in cunning, in revenge, in envy, in slander, in obscenity are at least as much involved in the expression of J's exuberance as they are of Homer's. But J's temporal nature is not Homer's spatial realm, and so the agonistic spirit manifests itself very differently in the linguistic universes of these two masters. In Homer, the gods transcend nature spatially, but Yahweh's transcendence is temporal. The overcoming of nature by means of the Blessing must be temporal also. Jacob's temporal victory over one of the Elohim is a curious kind of creative act which is one and the same as Jacob's cunning victories over Esau and Laban. In Greek terms this makes no sense, but in ancient Hebrew thinking this corresponds to that vision in which Yahweh's creation of the world, his rescue of the Israelites at the Red Sea, and the return of his people from Babylon are all one creative act on his part. Thorleif Boman defines the Hebrew word for eternity, *olam,* as meaning neither otherworldliness nor chronological infinity but rather time without boundaries. Something like that is the prize for which agonists strive in J. When Jacob becomes Israel, the implication is that his descendants also will prevail in a time without boundaries.

That Jacob is, throughout his life, an agonist, seems beyond dispute, and certainly was the basis for Thomas Mann's strong reading of J's text in the beautiful *Tales of Jacob* volume which is the glory of Mann's Joseph tetralogy. Yet distinguishing Hebrew from Greek agon is not much beyond a starting point in the interpretation of the recalcitrant originality of J's text. Whoever it is among the Elohim, the angel fears a catastrophe, and vainly inflicts a crippling wound upon Jacob, averting one catastrophe at the price of another. And yet, as agonists, the angel and Jacob create a blessing, the name of Israel, a name that celebrates the agonistic virtue of persistence, a persistence into unbounded temporality. That creation by catastrophe is one clear mark of this encounter. Another is the carrying across from Jacob's struggles in earlier life, veritably in the womb, his drive to have priority, where the carrying across is as significant as the drive. If the drive for priority is a version of what Freud has taught us to call family romance, then the conveyance of early zeal and affect into a later context is what Freud has taught us to call transference.

Catastrophe creation, family romance, and transference are a triad equally central to J and to Freud, and in some sense Freud's quest was to replace J and the other biblical writers as the legitimate exemplar of these paradigms. Ambivalence is the common element in the three paradigms, if we define ambivalence strictly as a contradictory stance mixing love and hate towards a particular object. Before returning to Wrestling Jacob, I want to cite the most shocking instance of Yahweh's ambivalence in the Hebrew Bible, an ambivalence manifested towards his particular favorite, Moses. The text is Exod. 4:24–26, translated literally:

Yahweh encountered Moses when Moses camped at night on his way
[to Egypt] and Yahweh sought to kill Moses. So Zipporah [Moses'
wife] cut off her son's foreskin with a flint and touched Moses on
his legs with it, saying: "Truly you are a bridegroom of blood to
me." And when Yahweh let Moses alone, she added, "A bridegroom
of blood due to the circumcision."

Confronted by this passage, normative interpretation has been very unhappy
indeed, since in it the uncanny of originality has gone beyond all limits. Indeed
only Gnostics, ancient and modern, could be happy with this text, in which
the agonistic seems truly to have crossed over into a really shocking divine
murderousness. Whoever it was among the Elohim, even if the Angel of Death,
Jacob undauntedly confronted an agonist. Yet Zipporah is even more courageous
in her rescue of Moses. Perhaps the Hebraic concept of agon is more extensive
even than I have indicated. Consider, though only briefly, the opening of Psalm
19, which I cite in the extraordinary King James version:

The heavens declare the glory of God; and the firmament showeth
his handiwork.
    Day unto day uttereth speech, and night unto night showeth
knowledge.
    There is no speech nor language, where their voice is not heard.
    Their line is gone out through all the earth, and their words to
the end of the world. In them hath he set a tabernacle for the sun,
    Which is as a bridegroom coming out of his chamber, and rejoiceth
as a strong man to run a race.
    His going forth is from the end of the heaven, and his circuit unto
the ends of it: and there is nothing hid from the heat thereof.

That marvelous fifth verse reverberates in Spenser, Shakespeare, Milton, and
Wordsworth, and is the most curiously Pindaric moment in the Bible, with the
Hebrew agonistic vision coinciding just this once with the Greek. But against
whom is this rejoicing bridegroom of a sun contending? Not with God but with
man, must be the answer. The Psalmist is far more normative than the Yahwist.
Who could conceive of a Psalm in the uncanny mode of the Yahwist? One way
of arriving at a reading of Wrestling Jacob's night encounter is to contrast it
with the characteristic stances and attitudes of the poets of Psalms confronting
their Maker. Voices in the Psalms do not demand blessings; they implore. The
sun emerges from his chamber like a bridegroom, and rejoicing at his own skill
as an agonist, but the sun reflects the glory of God. It is not God's glory but
Israel's, meaning Jacob just transformed into Israel, which is celebrated so sublimely by the Yahwist:

The sun rose upon him just as he passed Penuel, limping on his hip.

What allies Freud to the Yahwist is this agonistic Sublime, as manifested in the power of the uncanny, in what cannot be rendered normative. We might think of the school of Ego Psychology, of Heinz Hartmann, Lowenstein, Kris, and Erikson, as being Psalmists in relation to Freud-as-Yahwist, an analogy that could be continued by describing Lacan and his school as Gnostics. Scenes of Instruction like the agon of Jacob or Yahweh's night attack upon Moses are akin to Freud's fantasies of catastrophe, because the outrage to normative sensibilities is beyond assimilation. Even our difficulties in recovering the uncanny originality of J are matched by our difficulties in acknowledging how peculiar and extreme a writer Freud sometimes compels himself to be, for reasons nearly as unknowable as the Yahwist's motives.

Wittgenstein, who resented Freud, and who dismissed Freud as a mythologist, however powerful, probably was too annoyed with Freud to read him closely. This may explain Wittgenstein's curious mistake in believing that Freud had not distinguished between the Primal Scene and the somewhat later Primal Scene fantasy. Freud's Primal Scene takes place in the beginning, when an infant sees his parents in the act of love, without in any way understanding that sight. Memory, according to Freud, holds on to the image of copulation until the child, between the ages of three and five, creates the Primal Scene fantasy, which is an Oedipal reverie. One of my former students, Cathy Caruth, caught me in making this same error, so that in my literary transformation of Freud into the Primal Scene of Instruction, I referred to such a Primal Scene as being at once oral and written. I would clarify this now by saying that the "oral" scene is the topos or Primal Scene proper, the negative moment of being influenced, a perpetually lost origin, while the "written" scene is the trope or Primal Scene fantasy. This means, in my terms, that in a poem a topos or rhetorical commonplace is *where* something can be *known,* but a trope or inventive turning is *when* something is desired or *willed.* Poems, as I have written often, are verbal utterances that cannot be regarded as being simply linguistic entities, because they manifest their will to utter *within* traditions of uttering, and as soon as you will that "within," your mode is discursive and topological as well as linguistic and tropological. As a Primal Scene, the Scene of Instruction is a Scene of Voicing; only when fantasized or troped does it become a Scene of Writing.

That Scene of Voicing founds itself upon the three models of family romance, transference, and catastrophe creation, and here I assert no novelty in my own formulation, since Dryden for one deals with the family romance of poets in his *Preface to Fables, Ancient and Modern,* with poetic transference in stating his preference for Juvenal over Horace in his *Discourse Concerning . . . Satire,* and even with a kind of catastrophe creation in his *Parallel Betwixt Poetry and Painting.*

Dryden's mastery of dialectical contrasts between related poets seems to me now as good a guide for an antithetical practical criticism as I can find. Dryden is dialectical both in the open sense that Martin Price expounds, an empirical testing by trial and error, and also in the antithetical sense in which his description of one poet always points back to the contrasting poet from whom the critic is turning away.

What Dryden and the English tradition cannot provide is a third sense of critical dialectic, which in Freudian or Hegelian terms is the problematic notion of the overdetermination of language, and the consequent underdetermination of meaning. Hegelian terms do not much interest me, even in their Heideggerian and deconstructive revisions, since they seem to me just too far away from the pragmatic workings of poetry. Catastrophe creation, whether in its explicit Gnostic and Kabbalistic versions, or its implicit saga in the later Freud, contributes a model for distinguishing between the meaning of things in non-verbal acts, and the meaning of words in the linguistic and discursive acts of poetry. By uttering truths of desire within traditions of uttering, the poetic will also gives itself a series of overdetermined names. Gnosis and Kabbalah are attempts to explain how the overdetermination of Divine names has brought about an underdetermination of Divine meanings, a bringing about that is at once catastrophe and creation, a movement from fullness to emptiness.

Freud is not only the powerful mythologist Wittgenstein deplored, but also *the* inescapable mythologist of our age. His claims to science should be shrugged aside forever; that is merely his mask. Freudian literary criticism I remember comparing to the Holy Roman Empire: not holy, or Roman, or an empire; not Freudian, or literary, or criticism. Any critic, theoretical or practical, who tries to *use* Freud ends up being used *by* Freud. But Freud has usurped the role of the mind of our age, so that more than forty years after his death we have no common vocabulary for discussing the works of the spirit except what he gave us. Philosophers, hard or soft, speak only to other philosophers; theologians mutter only to theologians; our literary culture speaks to us in the language of Freud, even when the writer, like Nabokov or Borges, is violently anti-Freudian. Karl Kraus, being Freud's contemporary, said that psychoanalysis itself was the disease of which it purported to be the cure. We come after, and we must say that psychoanalysis itself is the culture of which it purports to be the description. If psychoanalysis and our literary culture no longer can be distinguished, then criticism is Freudian whether it wants to be or not. It relies upon Freudian models even while it pretends to be in thrall to Plato, Aristotle, Coleridge, or Hegel, and all that I urge is that it achieve a clearer sense of its bondage.

Freudian usurpation as a literary pattern is uniquely valuable to critics because it is *the* modern instance of poetic strength, of the agonistic clearing-away of cultural rivals, until the Freudian tropes have assumed the status of priority, while nearly all precedent tropes seem quite belated in comparison. When we think of earliness we now think in terms of primal repression, of the unconscious, of primary process, and of the drives or instincts, and all these are Freud's figurative language in his literary project of representing the civil wars of the psyche. The unconscious turns out alas not to be structured like *a* language, but to be structured like *Freud's* language, and the ego and superego, in their conscious aspects, are structured like Freud's own texts, for the very good reason that they *are* Freud's texts. We have become Freud's texts, and the *Imitatio Freudi* is the necessary pattern for the spiritual life in our time.

Ferenczi, a great martyr of that *Imitatio*, urged us in his apocalyptic *Thalassa*

> to drop once and for all the question of the beginning and end of life, and conceive the whole inorganic and organic world as a perpetual oscillating between the will to live and the will to die in which an absolute hegemony on the part of either life or death is never attained
> . . . it seems as though life had always to end catastrophically, even as it began, in birth, with a catastrophe.

Ferenczi is following yet also going beyond Freud's apocalyptic *Beyond the Pleasure Principle,* where the Nirvana Principle or Death Drive is described as an *"urge inherent in organic life to restore an earlier state of things* which the living entity has been obliged to abandon under the pressure of external disturbing forces." Such an urge, Freud insists, takes priority over the Pleasure Principle, and so *"the aim of all life is death."* Three years later, in *The Ego and the Id,* Freud speculated upon the two aboriginal catastrophes dimly repeated in every human development under the ill-starred dominance of the death drive. Our curious pattern of sexual development, particularly the supposed latency period between the ages of five and twelve, is related to those great cataclysms when all the cosmos became ice and again when the oceans went dry and life scrambled up upon the shore. These are Freud's scientistic versions of the Gnostic escapades of the Demiurge, or the great trope of the Breaking of the Vessels in the Lurianic Kabbalah.

But why should Freud have been haunted by images of catastrophe, however creative? It is not, I think, hyperbolic to observe that, for the later Freud, human existence is quite as catastrophic a condition as it was for Pascal and for Kierkegaard, for Dostoevsky and for Schopenhauer. There is a crack in everything that God has made, is one of Emerson's dangerously cheerful apothegms. In Freud, the fissure in us between primary process and secondary process insures that each of us is her or his own worst enemy, exposed endlessly to the remorseless attacks of the superego, whose relation to the hapless ego is shockingly like the Gnostic vision of the relation of Yahweh to human beings.

The horror of the family romance, as Freud expounds it, is one version of this human fissure, since the child attempts to trope one of the stances of freedom, yet makes the parents into the numinous shadows that Nietzsche called ancestor gods. As a revision of the Primal Scene, the family romance's falsification shows us that Oedipal fantasies are only ironies, or beginning moments merely, for truly strong poets and poems. This limitation makes the family romance a model neither catastrophic nor creative enough, and gives us the necessity for advancing to another model, the psychoanalytic transference, whose workings are closer to the dialectical crises of poetic texts.

The Freudian transference, as I have attempted to demonstrate elsewhere, depends for its pattern upon the sublimely crazy myth that Freud sets forth in *Totem and Taboo*. Briefly and crudely, the totem is the psychoanalyst and the taboo is the transference. All the ambivalences of the Oedipal situation are transferred from the individual's past to the analytical encounter, and the agon thus threatens to act out again the erotic defeat and tragedy of every psyche whatsoever. Against this threat, Freud sought to muster the strength of what he called "working through" but his beautiful late essay, "Analysis Terminable and Interminable," confesses that the benign powers of the totemic analyst tend to be confounded by the malign intensity of each patient's fantasy-making power. Working-through is replaced by repetition, and so by the death drive, which deeply contaminates all repressive defenses. This mutual contamination of drive and defense is the clearest link between Freud's visionary cosmos and the arena of Post-Enlightenment poetry. Contamination is not a trope but the necessary condition of all troping (or all defending); another word for contamination here might be "blurring" or even "slipping." There may be boundaries between the ego and the id, but they blur always in the transference situation, just as poet and precursor slip together in the Scene of Instruction or influence relationship.

I am suggesting that neither my use of Freud's images of Oedipal ambivalence, nor those images themselves, are generally read strongly enough. Identification in the Oedipal agon is not the introjection of the paternal superego but rather is a violent narcissistic metamorphosis. I rely here upon a formulation by the psychoanalyst Joseph H. Smith:

> The poet as poet is taken over by a power with which he has chosen to wrestle. It is not essentially a matter of passivity. The experience of a negative moment that coincides with the negative moment of a precursor is to be understood as an achieved catastrophe. It reaches beyond the ordinary understanding of oedipal identification to those primal internalizations which are and yet cannot be because no boundary is yet set across which anything could be said to be inter-

nalized. They are, rather, boundary-establishing phenomena which presuppose the possibility of internalization proper. But who is to say that there is not such a reestablishment of boundaries even in oedipal identifications?

I would go further than Smith in suggesting that every ambivalent identification with another self, writer or reader, parent or child, is an agon that makes ghostlier the demarcations between self and other. That blurring or slipping creates, in that it restores the abyss in the Gnostic sense, where the abyss is the true, alien godhead that fell away into time when the Demiurge sickened to a catastrophic false creation. The transference shakes the foundations of the ego more authentically than the family romance does, even though the transference is an artificial Eros and the family romance a natural one. After all, the transference, like a poem, is a lie against time, a resistance that must be overcome if we are to accept unhappy truth. Let us call a transference a kind of parody of a Sublime poem, since the taboo protects the totem analyst from the patient, yet no taboo can protect a precursor poet from the fresh strength or daemonic counter-sublime of an authentic new poet. To call a transference a parody of a poem is to suggest that catastrophe creations and family romances are also parodies of poetic texts. How can a parody be a model or paradigm for interpretation? We are accustomed to thinking of poems as parodies of prior poems, or even as parodies of paradigms. Yet reversing the order gets us closer, I am convinced, to the actualities of poetic interpretation.

Yeats wrote that "Plato thought nature but a spume that plays/Against a ghostly paradigm of things." Freud thought of nature very differently, yet he had his own version of a transcendentalism, in what he called "reality testing." Yet his paradigms for object attachments play uncanny tricks upon nature, or perhaps rely upon the uncanny tricks that nature seems to play with human sexuality. I go back here to the passages I quoted from the *Three Essays on the Theory of Sexuality* earlier in this chapter. The child sucking at his mother's breast becomes the paradigm for all sexual pleasure in later life, and Freud asserts that to begin with, sexual activity props itself upon the vital function of nourishment by the mother's milk. Thumb-sucking and the sensual smacking of the lips then give Freud the three characteristics of infantile sexual manifestation. These are: (1) Propping, at the origin, upon a vital somatic function; (2) auto-eroticism, or the lack of a sexual object; (3) domination of sexual aim by an erotogenic zone; here, the lips. It is at this point in his discussion that Freud makes one of his uncanniest leaps, relying upon his extraordinary trope of *Anlehnung* or propping (or anaclisis, as Strachey oddly chose to translate it). While the propping of the sexual drive upon the vital order still continues, the sexual drive finds its first object outside the infant's body in the mother's breast, and in the milk ensuing from it. Suddenly Freud surmises that just at the time the infant is capable of forming a total idea of the mother, quite abruptly the infant loses the initial object of the mother's breast, and tragically is thrown back upon auto-eroticism. Consequently, the sexual drive has no proper object again until after the latency period has transpired, and adolescence begins. Hence that dark and infinitely suggestive Freudian sentence: "The finding of an object is in fact a re-finding of it."

Thus human sexuality, alas, on this account has not had, from its very origins, any real object. The only real object was milk, which belongs to the vital order. Hence the sorrows and the authentic anguish of all human erotic quest, hopelessly seeking to rediscover an object, which never was the true object anyway. All human sexuality is thus tropological, whereas we all of us desperately need and long for it to be literal. As for sexual excitation, it is merely what Wrestling Sigmund terms a marginal effect (*Nebenwirkung*), because it reflects always the propping process, which after all has a double movement, of initial leaning, and then deviation or swerving. As Laplanche says, expounding Freud: "Sexuality in its entirety is in the slight deviation, the *clinamen* from the function." Or as I would phrase it, our sexuality is in its very origins a misprision, a strong misreading, on the infant's part, of the vital order. At the crossing (Laplanche calls it a "breaking or turning point") of the erotogenic zones, our sexuality is a continual crisis, which I would now say is not so much mimicked or parodied by the High Romantic crisis poem, but rather our sexuality itself is a mimicry or parody of the statelier action of the will which is figured forth in the characteristic Post-Enlightenment strong poem.

I call Freud, in the context of these uncanny notions, "Wrestling Sigmund," because again he is a poet of Sublime agon, here an agon between sexuality and the vital order. Our sexuality is like Jacob, and the vital order is like that one among the Elohim with whom our wily and heroic ancestor wrestled, until he had won the great name of Israel. Sexuality and Jacob triumph, but at the terrible expense of a crippling. All our lives long we search in vain, unknowingly, for the lost object, when even that object was a *clinamen* away from the true aim. And yet we search incessantly, do experience satisfactions, however marginal, and win our real if limited triumph over the vital order. Like Jacob, we keep passing Penuel, limping on our hips.

How can I conclude? Paradigms are not less necessary, but more so, when the power and the originality of strong poets surpass all measure, as Freud and the Yahwist go beyond all comparison. Sexuality, in Freud's great tropological vision, is at once a catastrophe creation, a transference, and a family romance. The Blessing, in the Yahwist's even stronger vision, is yet more a catastrophe creation, a transference, a family romance. Those strategems of the spirit, those stances and attitudes, those positions of freedom, or ratios of revision and crossings, that I have invoked as aids to reading strong poems of the Post-Enlightenment, are revealed as being not wholly inadequate to the interpretation of the Yahwist and of Freud. So I conclude with the assertion that strength demands strength. If we are to break through normative or weak misreadings of the Yahwist and of Freud, of Wordsworth and Whitman and Stevens, then we require strong paradigms, and these I have called upon agonistic tradition to provide.

Joseph, Judah, and Jacob

James S. Ackerman

Scholars have long noted the unusual amount of doubling in the Joseph story: three sets of dreams occur in pairs—by Joseph, by his fellow prisoners, and by Pharaoh. Joseph is twice confined—in the pit and in prison. The brothers make two trips to Egypt for grain, have two audiences with Joseph on each occasion, twice find money in their grain bags, make two attempts to gain Jacob's permission to send Benjamin to Egypt, and finally receive two invitations to settle in Egypt. Both Potiphar and the prison keeper leave everything in Joseph's hands. Potiphar's wife makes two attempts to seduce Joseph and then accuses him twice. Joseph serves two prominent prisoners (and two years elapse between their dreams and those of Pharaoh). Joseph twice accuses his brothers of spying, devises two plans to force the brothers to bring Benjamin to Egypt, and on two occasions places money in their sacks. Finally, the same goods (gum, balm, and myrrh) are twice brought from Canaan to Egypt—first with Joseph and later with Benjamin.

Doubling appears in speeches as well as actions. In some instances characters repeat a phrase in one episode (e.g., Gen. 41:25, 28; 42:15, 16; 43:3, 5). Elsewhere, speeches recapitulate and supplement events reported earlier in the story (e.g., Gen. 40:15; 42:21–22; 42:31–34; 43:7; 43:20–23; 44:3–7; 44:18–34; 50:17).

The common assumption has been that much of the doubling is a result of the conflation of sources—an assumption I shall not question here. My concern is to point out the effect that doubling has as a literary device in the story. D. B. Redford, for example, has noted that doubling can often be used for emphasis: "The certainty of the dreams' fulfillment is thus stressed, as well as the stubborn-

From *Literary Interpretations of Biblical Narratives*. Vol. 2. © 1982 by Abingdon Press.

ness of Jacob, Joseph's determination to treat his brothers as spies, Egyptian initiative in making possible Israel's settlement in Egypt, and so on." A second effect of doubling, Redford believes, is plot retardation in some crucial instances. For example, while the doublets are emphasizing Jacob's stubbornness and Joseph's determination, they are also delaying the recognition scene in which the brothers will discover the identity of the Egyptian lord.

Acknowledging the many instances of these kinds of doubling, I would argue that there is a deeper, structural doubling in the Joseph story — occasioned by the unexpected turn of events in chapter 42 when the brothers first come to Egypt to bring grain. "And Joseph's brothers came, and they did obeisance to him — nostrils to the ground."* (All asterisked biblical quotations have been made directly from the Hebrew text.) This is the outcome envisioned in Joseph's first dream of ascendancy over the rest of the family (Gen. 37:5-7). We hadn't known what to make of those dreams: had special favor been thrust on the youth, or did he grasp after it by tattling on his brothers? Did the dreams indicate divine choice, or were they the ambitious imaginings of a lad who would play the role of deity? Like Day Star, who had tried to replace the deity, Joseph is cast into the pit (Isa. 14:12ff); and then he is taken down into Egypt. But a recurring motif is God's presence with Joseph in Egypt, whether he is in Potiphar's house or in Pharaoh's prison. The reader notes with satisfaction that Joseph's rise to power in Egypt results from a combination of pious behavior, divine help, and his wise advice at court.

When the brothers come to Egypt for grain, the reader is prepared for the denouement. When they do obeisance before Joseph, we remember the dreams before he does. We assume that the story will soon end, showing how human beings cannot thwart the divine purpose. We have been prepared for this conclusion by chapter 41: after hearing and interpreting Pharaoh's dreams, Joseph tells him that the matter is fixed by God when a second dream repeats the first (Gen. 41:32). Then, as Joseph predicted, the seven-year cycles of plenty and drought take place. Thus as the brothers fulfill Joseph's dreams by bowing down before him, the lesson of God's control of history is played out again, and the reader may consider the main story at an end.

The denouement does not fulfill our expectations, however, as Joseph turns with apparent vengeance on his brothers. Scholars who question Joseph's morality or who see him reverting to his earlier adolescent behavior are overlooking a literary device used by the storyteller: "And Joseph recognized his brothers; but as for them, they did not recognize him. And Joseph *remembered the dreams* that he had dreamed about them. And he said to them, 'Spies you are — to see the nakedness of the land' "* (Gen. 42:8-9a).

At this crucial moment of confrontation, the prostrated brothers bring to his mind an image from the past. Like the reader, Joseph remembers not the betrayal or suffering wrought by his brothers, but his dreams. We have been seduced by the baker-butler and the Pharaoh dream sequences into assuming that dreams indicate that what has been fixed by God will inevitably come to pass. Here is the climactic instance: Joseph's brothers are bowing down before him. We are not prepared for further plot complications.

In the unusual description of Joseph's thoughts in Gen. 42:9, the syntax connects his remembering the dreams with his accusing his brothers, launching a new series of events. That syntactical connection suggests that everything that follows is related to his dreams. We have just been told how Joseph, in naming his Egyptian-born sons, had put the past behind him: "God has made me forget all my hardship and all my father's house [and] made me fruitful in the land of my affliction" (Gen. 41:51, 52). Now events remind him of his dreams. And somehow, from Joseph's point of view, the dreams have not yet been *completely* fulfilled.

As we read further it quickly becomes clear that Joseph's immediate purpose is to have the brothers bring Benjamin to Egypt. Then we recall: *all* the brothers' sheaves had bowed to Joseph's sheaf, and Benjamin is still in Canaan. The lad must join the brothers in Joseph's presence. And Joseph must continue to dissemble, since the first dream depicts his being treated as lord rather than brother.

We might wonder why Joseph focuses on bringing only Benjamin to Egypt. He does ask after Jacob's welfare, but makes no effort to include the patriarch in his machinations with his brothers. When we look more closely at Joseph's dreams, however, we see that they were not so closely doubled as were Pharaoh's. The motif of obeisance appears in both dreams; but the first points only to the brothers, while the second includes the whole family. Thus Joseph's dream sequence establishes the pattern for his course of action after his brothers come to Egypt: obeisance of all the brothers is of first importance.

Joseph may not yet be conscious of the full meaning of his dreams. With the dreams of the butler-baker and Pharaoh, the pattern had been dream-interpretation-fulfillment. In Joseph's own case, however, the interpretation will not be clear to him until after the dreams have been fulfilled — possibly because he himself must play a role in bringing the dreams to fulfillment.

Both the recognition of the brothers and the recollection of the dreams are one-sided. As a plot device, they force the reader to see what follows in the light of what has preceded. But what of the actors in this drama? Will Joseph come to understand the connection between his dreams and the new sequence of events? Will the brothers come to the same understanding? Will they not have to relive Joseph's suffering so they can fully realize what they did to him?

The brothers soon recall their past crime and interpret their present misfortunes as a long-delayed retribution, but there is room for further growth. Joseph recalls his dreams, but is not yet able to interpret their meaning. Thus after the climactic meeting the story is so arranged that Joseph, in acting out his dreams, will embark on a twice-told tale through which he will both fulfill and learn the divine purpose for his life.

One result of this plot device is a series of dramatic ironies, some apparent to Joseph, some appreciated only by the reader:

(a) "We are all sons of one man," say the brothers in Gen. 42:11, not realizing that their statement includes the strange lord standing before them.

(b) "You will be tested. . . . Send one of you and let him bring your brother . . . so that your words may be tested, whether *'emet* [a word that means both *truth* and *faithfulness*] is with you,"* says Joseph in 42:15–16. The brothers pass half of the test in chapter 43. There was *'emet/truth* with them: they have proved they were the family unit they had claimed to be, rather than a group of spies, by producing the youngest son. But they will soon discover that the test has not ended. It is yet to be determined whether or not *'emet/faithfulness* was with them.

(c) When Jacob finally relents and agrees to send Benjamin, he prays in 43:14 that God will prosper the journey "so that he will send to you your brother, another, and Benjamin."* The father may be referring to Simeon, the brother kept hostage in Egypt. But Jacob did not say "your other brother." The syntax leaves the meaning just ambiguous enough for the reader to know that it can also refer to Joseph.

(d) In 42:21 we are told that Joseph had earlier pleaded for "favor" (*ḥnn*) for himself, but his brothers would not listen. When Joseph first meets Benjamin, he gives the pious, traditional greeting "May God grant you favor [*ḥnn*], my son"* (43:29). Those words will have a deeper significance as the plot develops. Will the other son of Rachel find "favor" from the brothers when they are asked to leave him enslaved in Egypt and return to their father?

(e) When the brothers return to the Egyptian lord after the divining cup has been discovered in Benjamin's sack, Judah's defense should be nolo contendere: they cannot defend themselves against the charge, even though they consider themselves not guilty. Instead, however, Judah exclaims, "God has found out the guilt of your servants" (44:16). Does he mean that the Egyptian should accept the statement as an admission of guilt regarding a deliberate theft, or something else? The guilt that Judah acknowledges God has "found out"—we and his brothers know—is for an incident that took place long ago.

A second result of the narrative device of delayed fulfillment is the doubled plot. Readers can see the brothers suffering, in part at least, measure for measure for what they did in the past:

(a) In Genesis 37, as Joseph approached his brothers in Dothan, "they *saw* him . . . and they conspired [*vayyitnakkĕlû*] against him." Finally they returned with the bloody garment to their father, saying "This we have found; *recognize* now — cloak of your son — is it or not?"* Twenty years later, when the brothers first appear before Joseph, "he *saw* his brothers, and he *recognized* them; but he acted unrecognizably [*vayyitnakkēr*] unto them"* — the significant pun, in a technique characteristic of the whole story, reinforcing the moral pattern of measure for measure. Joseph's dissembling echoes the brothers' conspiring. In 37:4 "they were not able to speak peaceably to him."* Now Joseph "speaks harshly to them"* (42:7). Those who had duped their father into "recognition" are now recognized. The deceivers are deceived. The ones who had seen Joseph and conspired against him are now on the receiving end, and the key to the deception is Joseph "acting unrecognizably."

(b) Joseph then falsely accuses the brothers of coming "to see the nakedness of the land"* (42:9). In the biblical tradition "nakedness" consistently occurs in texts referring to sexual misconduct. Are we not being asked to recall Joseph's plight in Genesis 39, when Potiphar's wife falsely accused him of sexual misconduct, causing his angry master to throw him in prison? Now Joseph falsely accuses his brothers and has them bound over into prison for a period of three days.

(c) In 40:15 Joseph, interpreting the butler's dream, uses language that equates his Egyptian imprisonment with an earlier event in his life: "For I was indeed stolen from the land of the Hebrews, and also here I have not done anything that they should place me *in the pit*."* Joseph is linking his brothers' betrayal with his imprisonment, so that the memory of his suffering is doubly tied to the pit. Thus when he imprisons his brothers, he is forcing them to relive two separate experiences from the past: his imprisonment by Potiphar, and his being cast into the pit by his brothers.

(d) While in prison, the brothers must decide which one will return to tell Jacob that nine more of his sons have been taken and that Benjamin must also come down to Egypt; they realize that Jacob will hold back. Desolately, the brothers in the prison/pit contemplate the prospect of death or slavery — just as Joseph had earlier sat in their pit awaiting death. He is meting out, measure for measure, what he had suffered in the past.

The outburst of "measure for measure" activity soon ends. After three days Joseph changes his mind and allows the brothers to return to Canaan, keeping only Simeon as a hostage. Why do we find the seemingly unnecessary change of plan after this short interval? Joseph's first response to his brothers had been punitive. He had wanted his brothers to relive in part the hardships that he had experienced. But his major purpose is to bring his dreams to fulfillment, and this necessitates a change in strategy. He also must realize that sending only one brother back home would be a certain overkill that would cause Jacob to dig in his heels, frustrating his intention. Thus he carefully modifies his course of action.

This change initiates a chain of events that will be part of a third plot doubling. The result of Joseph's changed course of action is to bring the brothers' long-repressed guilt to the surface. Only now will there be discussion and recriminations among them concerning what had happened twenty years before. Why does this happen? It is unclear whether Joseph intends it or not, but the changed course of action—ostensibly aimed at fulfilling the dreams—is subtly forcing the brothers to relive their earlier crime. Thus with Gen. 42:18ff we move from a "measure for measure" punitive reaction to a more subtle "play within a play" in which, like Hamlet's uncle, the brothers will be forced to relive the past and face its horror.

The first expression of guilt comes as soon as they learn that they must return to their father to fetch Benjamin (42:21–22). Why is this? Surely part of the reason is a growing sense of déjà vu among the brothers. They must return to their father with the dreadful news of a second lost brother—this time, Simeon; and at the same time they must demand that Jacob surrender the other son of Rachel. Their imprisonment had forced them to relive Joseph's pit/imprisonment experiences. Now they must reenact their earlier crime.

On the homeward journey one of the brothers discovers silver in his sack. "What is this that God had done to us?" they exclaim. They are horrified by the discovery of what, in other circumstances, could have been construed as an act of kindness. Surely, their reaction is to some extent caused by fear that the money is part of a setup: it will be used as an occasion for a second false accusation that will result in imprisonment, slavery, or death when they return to Egypt. But the silver gained in the context of losing another brother also echoes their grim plan to sell Joseph into slavery for silver. That time, the Midianites had foiled their plan and received the silver instead. Now as the brothers return to their father minus another brother and with silver in their sacks, we (and possibly also the brothers) may well feel that the payoff for their earlier crime was twenty years delayed in coming.

The brothers have changed. As the story repeats itself, we must notice the great difference between their attitude toward Jacob's suffering over the report of Joseph's loss with the bloody garment and their description of why Simeon was taken and what they must do with Benjamin. They are now sincere, compassionate for their mourning father, desperate to set things straight. Reuben offers the lives of his two sons if Benjamin does not return. But Jacob pitifully turns them away. If Benjamin is lost, "you would bring my gray hairs in sorrow to Sheol."* This echoes Jacob's response to the loss of Joseph: "I will go down to my son mourning—to Sheol"* (37:35).

The parallels continue, as the reader picks up an irony that must elude the brothers. Jacob, after a long struggle, has finally been convinced that the family will not survive if Benjamin is not sent to Egypt. The wily father hopes for the best and does what he can by sending gifts to the Egyptian lord (43:11). Thus Benjamin departs for Egypt; and with him go balm, honey, gum, myrrh, pistachio nuts, and almonds — the very goods that accompanied Joseph twenty years before (37:25). The brothers had been indirectly responsible for Joseph's earlier descent into Egypt. This time they must take Benjamin in their own caravan. The allusion to the items of transport suggests that this time the brothers are reenacting the role of the Ishmaelite traders, bringing the other son of Rachel to an uncertain fate.

When the brothers arrived in Egypt with Benjamin, "they did obeisance before him to the ground"* (43:26). With this statement, the narrator stresses that the first dream has been completely fulfilled. We can assume the same of the divine purpose contained in the dream. As for Joseph's own reported purpose, the brothers have demonstrated that *'emet* is with them by producing Benjamin; they have told the truth. Joseph generously provides a banquet for his brothers; and they all feast, drink, even become drunk together. As chapter 43 draws to a close, the writer would have a perfect opportunity to describe Joseph's revelation of his true identity; but Joseph bypasses it.

Why not tell all right now? Joseph proceeds on a course of action that is puzzling (why pick on Benjamin, the one innocent brother?) and that goes beyond the dreams. We should remember, however, that Pharaoh's dreams told only what was fixed by God: seven years of plenty, followed by seven years of famine. They did not hint at the appropriate mode of human response to the fixed divine action, so that the human community would gain the maximum benefit. The appropriate response required a discreet and wise person in whom was the spirit of God. Similarly, Joseph's dreams had disclosed only the course of events that God would ultimately bring about within the family of Jacob: the young Joseph would rise to ascendancy over his brothers and parents. His dreams did not disclose the appropriate response to what they foretold. May we not assume that, as Joseph's response to Pharaoh's dreams had benefited all of Egypt in chapter 41, his mysterious course of action with the divining cup in chapter 44 will somehow benefit the family of Israel?

The first allusion to Joseph's dreams in Gen. 42:8-9 begins a plot doubling in which the brothers go through two distinct stages:

A. Measure for measure. First they suffer fit retribution for their crime against Joseph and for his tribulations in the land of Egypt — false accusation and imprisonment, with the fear of death or slavery.

B. Reenactment of the crime. As they return to their father minus a brother and with silver in their sack, hear their father's renewed anguish, and bring the second son of Rachel into Egypt, they are forced to relive painful scenes from the past that bring their guilt to the surface.

Both stages take place as part of Joseph's need to bring his dream to fulfillment. Note also that the brothers' experience is the chronological reverse of the earlier plot: first they suffer what had happened to Joseph during and after the crime; then they relive the crime. Gen. 43:26 describes the literal fulfilling of Joseph's dream and initiates the final doubling that must precede the great climax and denouement of the story. In Aristotle's terms, we have had the major reversal and a one-sided recognition scene. Yet to come are the full recognition scene ("I am Joseph") and the final working out of the plot.

The third stage of the doubling is carefully planned to push events back to the point before the crime took place. When the brothers return to the Egyptian lord after the divining cup has been discovered in Benjamin's sack, the chronology has suddenly shifted. They are no longer acting out an earlier crime. Instead, they are given a chance to commit a new one. The plot doubling has structured events so that history can repeat itself and they can again be rid of the favored son. This time, however, they will be guiltless. All they have to do is go home and tell their father exactly what happened. Despite Judah's offer that all the brothers remain enslaved, Joseph tells them to return to their father "in peace." They surely recall Jacob's reaction to the loss of Joseph and their fruitless efforts to console him; the loss of the only other son of Rachel would destroy their father. Realization of this leads to Judah's moving speech in which he offers himself as a slave in Benjamin's stead so that the younger brother can return to his father.

When Joseph saw his eleven brothers bowed before him in 43:26, he knew that the divine plan foreshadowed in his first dream had been fulfilled. As a youth he could not have known why his ascendancy to power would be an important part of the divine plan to keep alive the family of Israel. As Joseph proceeds with the divining cup ruse, the narrative gives no indication that he has plumbed the relationship between his past suffering and his present power. Joseph's ploy with the divining cup is in no way related to the explanation he finally expresses to his brothers in 45:5-7. In chapter 44 Joseph's motivation is to test his brothers. They have proved their 'emet/truthfulness by producing Benjamin. Now he wants to learn whether they have grown and changed— whether there is the possibility of reestablishing brotherhood with them. (Paradoxically, as the brothers pass the test, Joseph will learn more than he had expected. Judah's speech will give him the key for interpreting the mystery of his own life. We will return to this later.)

The first dream has been fulfilled in 43:26, but the blessing of reconciliation among the brothers has not been realized. In this story a wise, human response is required to complement and complete the divine activity. Thus, structurally, the divining cup incident is to the fulfillment of Joseph's first dream what the construction of store-cities was to Pharaoh's dreams. The store-cities will contain the blessing of the harvest; the divining cup is the final test of *'emet/faithfulness* that, if passed, may bring the blessing of reconciliation among brothers.

Although the dominant theme of this story may be the providential care of the family of Israel through Joseph's career, reconciliation among brothers is a strong and closely related sub-theme: family survival involves both escape from famine and reconciliation among brothers. In chapter 37 the brothers were angry at Joseph when he tattled and jealous when he received the special garment — "they hated him, and could not *speak peaceably* to him" (37:4). These feelings were intensified by Joseph's dreams (37:5, 8, 11). The narrator reports no word spoken to Joseph as they cast him into the pit. In fact, when the brothers recall that incident in 42:21-22, they describe it as not listening to his entreaties.

The alienation theme is continued on Joseph's part as he "*speaks harshly*"* to his brothers when they first come down to Egypt (42:7); and in their first four encounters they are separated by an interpreter. The descriptions of Joseph's weeping indicate a gradual change in his attitude toward his brothers as he perceives that they have changed. But even in the banquet scene, which might have made a fitting climax, the narrator stresses the physical separation of Joseph from his brothers (43:32). They sat "before him." The language suggests a royal court in which the brothers are placed in subservient positions to the ruler. Even the phrase "They drank and became drunken with him [*'immô*]"* suggests the same court background. The brothers are together, but they are not a family. Only after they have passed the test in chapter 44 does reconciliation begin: "And he kissed all his brothers, and he wept upon them. And after that his brothers *spoke with* him" (45:15).

It had been Joseph's reports of his dreams that exacerbated the brothers' ill will toward the youth. They had interpreted the dreams as both a claim to divine favor and a sign of an overweening pride that was nurtured by Jacob's special love for Joseph. They naturally refused to see anything providential in a plan that would cast them down before any brother. There was a strong antimonarchical strand in early Israelite history, shaped by centuries of oppression at the hands of rulers who claimed to be benevolent shepherds of their people. The last thing that Joseph can do, if he wants to reestablish his place as brother in the family, is to overwhelm his brothers with his power. Conversely, the brothers must pass the divining-cup test so that Joseph can again become a brother and part of the family.

The theme of favoritism producing conflict runs throughout the book of

Genesis. At the human level it begins in the rivalry between Sarah and Hagar, forcing Abraham to favor Isaac and drive out Ishmael. It continues in the rivalry between Isaac's sons, Jacob and Esau — each favored by one parent. The struggle between brothers continues in the next generation, caused in large part by Jacob's special love for Rachel and her offspring over Leah and hers. In all these stories the younger son wins out over the older, and geographical separation helps resolve the conflict. Ishmael becomes a wilderness dweller as he and Hagar disappear from the story. Jacob flees to Haran, at Rebekah's behest, so that Esau will have time to forget what was done to him. When the brothers again meet twenty years later, Esau has indeed forgotten. He falls upon Jacob's neck and kisses him. Then each brother departs to his own special country.

The Joseph story continues these themes and brings them to a new resolution. Favoritism and deception play crucial roles in chapter 37. Like Sarah and Isaac, Rachel and her sons are the husband/father's favorites. As with the three earlier sets of brothers, parental favoritism sets up serious sibling rivalries. As with favoritism, so with deception. Just as Isaac had been unable to recognize (nkr) the disguised son he was blessing, Jacob, who had deceived his father and won that blessing, was himself deceived by his sons when he recognized (nkr) Joseph's bloodied garment and drew the wrong conclusions. Joseph also lived separated from his brothers for twenty years and finally had forgotten all his hardship and all his father's house (41:51). But at the crucial time of confrontation Joseph remembers his dreams and undertakes a series of actions that eventually results in reconciliation among the brothers. This reconciliation, however, will not be an uneasy peace best preserved by geographical separation. It is a reconciliation that results in the geographical reunification of the family of Israel.

It is a commonplace that Genesis 1–11 provides the prologue to introduce the story of Israel by depicting the ever-increasing alienation within the human community. Humankind had been created to live in Eden, in close proximity to God. Genesis 11 ends with a fragmented humanity — scattered and no longer able to understand one another's tongue.

One might assume that when Abraham is introduced, the story will describe how God begins to overcome the alienation among humans through the covenant community of Israel. But strangely the rivalry and hatred among brothers that had begun with Cain and Abel are continued within the family of Abraham. In fact, these themes that were present but muted in the generation of Isaac and Ishmael become increasingly intensified, culminating when the sons of Jacob behold the approaching "master dreamer" and determine that he shall die.

Paradoxically, divine favor has played a crucial role from the beginning in catalyzing the conflict among the brothers. We first note its appearance as God prefers Abel's sacrifice to Cain's. In the story of Israel divine favor is carried out through a parent. Abraham is driven to heed Sarah's words and turn against Ishmael when he learns that Isaac will be the child of promise. Rebekah's special love for Jacob may be traced directly to God's decree, given to her alone, that the second-born will ultimately prevail over the first-born. Divinely inspired dreams, given to a younger son who wears a special garment, continue and intensify the theme of divine and parental favoritism that produces conflict.

In Genesis 45 the conflict of brothers begins to be resolved. The brothers, through Judah's bold action in Genesis 44, have passed the crucial test. When they discover Joseph's true identity, he is no longer a vengeful sovereign for them but a brother; more important, he is not a vengeful brother but a forgiving brother. They have earned forgiveness for their crime against their brother.

Full reconciliation, however, cannot take place until they can resolve the issue that had partially instigated that crime: divine favoritism. Only when Joseph explains that the dreams indicated a specially ordained family role rather than a personally privileged divine love are the brothers able to approach him. Only when they perceive that Joseph's suffering and survival had played a key role in continued life for the family of Jacob-Israel are they able to "speak with him." The survival of the family had been the key issue in Judah's entreaty to Jacob to send Benjamin with them to Egypt. And the survival of Jacob-Israel had been the key theme in Judah's desperate plea before the Egyptian lord. The brothers have come in the course of the story to choose unity over separation, even if it means a shared slavery that could easily be avoided. They have also changed from a hatred that wills death for a favored one to an urgent concern for the life of the entire family. In fact, it is Judah's stress on the survival of "the little ones" — the next generation — that finally moves Jacob to risk the death of his last beloved son, Benjamin.

I have tried to show how the divining-cup incident in Genesis 44 is the culmination of the plot-doubling device begun in chapter 42. It places the brothers in a position of having to choose whether or not to repeat their crime of Genesis 37. Will yet another favored brother be sacrificed, escalating the danger to the life of Jacob-Israel—both as father and as symbol of family cohesion? Their action indicates that they now prefer the life and survival of all over the death/cutting off of any. The long history of the sibling rivalry motif that began with Cain and Abel was introduced into the Joseph story by 37:4 ("but when his brothers saw that their father loved him more than all his brothers, they hated him . . . "). It now moves toward resolution as they fall on one anothers' necks and kiss one another. The Babel motif of alienation resulting in a breakdown of communication, also introduced into the Joseph story in 37:4 ("and [they] could not speak peaceably to him"*) and intensified by the role of the court interpreter, moves toward resolution as "after this his brothers spoke with him"* (45:15).

The remainder of this [essay] will discuss another key doubling in the Joseph story: Reuben/Judah. Many scholars see both playing the "good brother" role in Genesis 37. In the original version there was one good brother, they claim, and the present confusion in the text results from a conflation of sources. Redford goes on to say, in fact, that Judah's role is not only a secondary intrusion into the narrative, but it also represents a diminution of the story's overall literary artistry. There may indeed be a conflation of sources, but I will argue that the redactor displays great artistry. In the final redaction Reuben and Judah play contrasting roles. Whereas Reuben will gradually weaken and disappear as the story unfolds, Judah will undergo the most important change of any of the characters so that he will play *the* key role in catalyzing the reconciliation. To what extent has the narrative prepared us for Judah's dramatic rise in Genesis 43–44?

Reuben, the first-born, is described as the good son in chapter 37. When the brothers see Joseph coming in the distance and plan to kill him, it is Reuben who seeks to foil the plan. Whereas the brothers plot a violent death for Joseph, Reuben sets limits: "let us not smite a life."* Acceding to part of the brothers' plan, he suggests that Joseph be thrown into a nearby pit alive rather than dead. The basis for his request is the prohibition against shedding blood. But the text makes clear that Reuben's interest is to rescue Joseph and restore him to his father. When the unexpected intervention of Midianites foils Reuben's plan, he bursts out in lamentation for himself: "and I, where shall I go?" (37:30). This may mean merely, "How can I face my father?" But might he see himself as banned fugitive, unable to return to his father because he has not lived up to the responsibility of first-born in protecting his brother?

Judah, the fourth-born of Leah, plays a role that sets him in contrast with Reuben. The text makes no mention that Judah's interest is to rescue Joseph. Instead Judah piously speaks of not laying a hand on a brother; but the effect of his suggestion is not so different from murder: Joseph will be removed from their midst and reduced to slavery. In many ways biblical law equates selling a person into slavery with murder. Judah wants the same results as his other brothers, but he seeks profit from the deed (37:26–27).

Both plans — Reuben's to save and Judah's to profit — are foiled. Out of nowhere come the Midianites, and in a half verse they carry out the action contemplated by the brothers. Like the nameless stranger who met Joseph at Shechem and told him his brothers had moved on to Dothan, the Midianites are mere agents of the plot. They appear suddenly in the story to foil the opposing machinations of Reuben and Judah and disappear after they have served their function.

N. Leibowitz, backed by midrashic interpretation, sees Joseph's nameless stranger as a divine emissary. Given the normal economy in biblical narrative style, there seems to be no need to tell us that Joseph was sent first to Shechem but then redirected to Dothan. Like the Midianites, the stranger appears from nowhere. He engages Joseph in a conversation that could easily have been omitted, and then he disappears from the story. Leibowitz infers that the narrator is going out of his way to emphasize the divine intent behind Joseph's fateful encounter with his brothers. I would argue the same thing for the role of the Midianites. They frustrate the plans of Reuben and Judah, but their sudden intervention into and disappearance from the story may cause us to anticipate that a larger plan, not yet revealed to characters or reader, is being carried out.

One must examine the larger context of the Joseph story to determine why Reuben and Judah play these opposing roles. Deriving his line of argument from midrashic interpretations, J. Goldin points us in a fruitful direction by referring to Genesis 34–35. In 35:22 we learn that Reuben had sexual relations with his father's concubine, Bilhah. He may have been attempting to assert the rights of primogeniture and assume the role of the father, but we learn from Gen. 49:3–4 that in fact his premature action had caused him to lose this status in his father's eyes. Goldin suggests that, besides fulfilling his special responsibility as first-born, Reuben may have been desperately attempting to regain his lost/threatened status by saving Joseph's life. When Reuben finds the pit empty, his response, as translated by Goldin, is "what now is left me" (37:30b). This alternate translation, like the conventional translation used above, leaves Reuben bemoaning his own fate as a response to Joseph's tragedy.

What about Judah, the fourth-born? His star may be on the rise. Levi and Simeon, the second- and third-born sons, had fallen from favor through their deceitful destruction of the city of Shechem (Genesis 34). Jacob rebukes them for their recklessness (34:30) and refers to it again in Gen. 49:5–7 in declaring their reduced status. Judah is next in line. If he stays out of trouble, and if Reuben does not regain favor, the special status of family leadership may fall to him. The only remaining rival is Joseph, the son favored by his father. Thus not only does the larger context of Genesis 37 show us how important it is for Reuben to save Joseph and return him to his father; it also reveals how much Judah stands to gain by being rid of the only other rival for special status among his brothers.

When the harsh-speaking Egyptian lord begins to test the brothers in chapter 42, Reuben still appears to be the "good brother." But there are now further ambiguities: his goodness has even more self-centeredness than before. The brothers speak with one accord in remembering and repenting their guilt; they admit that they did not heed Joseph's appeals for mercy. Only Reuben breaks the brothers' eloquent solidarity. Shrilly he turns on them with an "I told you so," refusing to accept the guilt while recognizing that he must share the judgment. The brothers remember not heeding Joseph. Reuben attempts to identify himself with the innocent, wronged younger brother—reminding them that they also did not heed him earlier. But they had indeed followed his lead in chapter 37. It was Reuben's advice to throw Joseph into the pit, as part of his plan to save the lad and return him to his father. Reuben's goodness was ineffective. His plan did not work, and we learn later that if it had worked, Jacob's family would not have survived the famine. As chapter 37 concluded, we found Reuben proclaiming his tragic isolation. The brothers did not heed his words, probably because of their irrelevance to the problem of explaining Joseph's disappearance to their father.

Reuben's goodness is similarly ineffective in chapter 42. The threatening situation before the Egyptian lord did not require a querulous expression of innocence that resulted in division and recrimination. The true first-born should provide leadership that assumed at least a shared responsibility for the situation. He should be the spokesman, coming up with an imaginative response to the Egyptian lord's accusation that would enhance the unity of the family and deliver the brothers from their peril. His lack of leadership here is a foil for the later doubling situation. Chapter 44 will portray another brother taking action before the Egyptian lord in even more threatening circumstances with vastly different results; and the reader is forced to compare the two spokesmen in these analogous situations.

When the brothers return to Jacob and describe their Egyptian adventures, they try to soften the severity of their position. Simeon is not a hostage bound over into prison, but simply a brother left to stay with the Egyptian. There was no threat of death to Simeon for failure to bring Benjamin to Egypt—only the promise to hand over Simeon and to allow the brothers to purchase grain in Egypt. The aged Jacob's response to this news is full of self-pitying, ineffective recrimination. After twenty years he still grieves for Joseph. Because he fears for Benjamin's life, he is incapable of an imaginative response. Here Reuben steps forward, making a statement more reckless than Jephthah's, offering the lives of two sons as pledge for Benjamin's.

Reuben's language reminds readers of his earlier intent "to *bring him* [Joseph] *unto* his father"* (37:22). In chapter 42 the same words are used to express Reuben's promise regarding Benjamin: "two of my sons you may kill if I do not *bring him unto* you"* (42:37). We know that Reuben tried and failed before. If Reuben fails again, his suggested resolution will wreak further death in Jacob's family. Many years ago Jacob had jumped to secure the birthright of Esau—the foolish, impulsive first-born. Now as a father he must be haunted to see Esau's traits reappear in his first-born, Reuben—so desperate to win favor that he will risk cutting off his own descendants. Jacob's impulse is to refuse, to cut his losses and take no further risk of lives in the family. Simeon's fate remains in abeyance until the grain sacks are emptied as the famine continues.

When the famine had first hit, Jacob had been quick to seize the initiative in preserving life among the family (42:1–2). The key words here are "so that we might live and not die."* The brothers, on the other hand, are depicted as "staring at each other," helpless and paralyzed, incapable of taking productive measures. Now in chapter 43 we see a feeble, pitiful old man, unwilling to risk Benjamin's life, begging his sons to "return, bring for us a little food."* With the wisdom of the senile, he does not mention Benjamin, hoping that his sons have forgotten the awful terms. Perhaps they can secure a few scraps without risking Benjamin's life. At this point Judah intervenes to make things clear to his father. Joseph had told the brothers that if they did not bring Benjamin with them they would die (42:20). He knew that the famine would continue and that the brothers would be forced to return to Egypt to survive. Judah had understood Joseph's meaning precisely, and he twice repeats that if they do not bring Benjamin they will not have access to the Egyptian who is the sole dispenser of the grain.

Judah has become the spokesman and leader. The main turning point is reached, however, when Judah offers to assume personal responsibility for Benjamin's life in verses 8–10. Just as chapter 37 forced us to contrast the two brothers' attempts to deliver Joseph from death, the analogy between the offers of Reuben and Judah to be responsible for Benjamin forces us to contrast their words in order to see why Reuben's offer hardened Jacob's resolve not to send Benjamin, whereas Judah's words won him over. Unlike Reuben, Judah is successful because he sets Jacob's decision in a larger context. He sees clearly that the continuation of the whole family is at stake, and he is able to get this insight through to his father by picking up and building on the same phrase Jacob had used in 42:2 to respond to the famine: "*so that we might live and not die*—also we, also you, also our offspring."* Whereas Reuben offered to destroy part of the next generation if he could not return Benjamin to his father, Judah emphasizes the necessity that the next generation must continue. He shows Jacob that Jacob's efforts to save the life of the younger, favored son are threatening the continuation of the entire line. How was Judah led to that conclusion?

Although the midrashic tradition was aware of many of the parallels between Genesis 37 and 38, Robert Alter has demonstrated how these parallels create a new literary unity, integrating the themes of the Judah-Tamar story into the Joseph narrative. Alter concentrates primarily on the integration between chapter 38 and chapters 37–39 of *Leitwörter*, images, and themes: Judah goes down from his brothers and Joseph is brought down to Egypt; Jacob mourns for "dead" Joseph, and Judah mourns for his dead sons; the brothers send the bloodied garment—"Please recognize . . . "*—to unmask deception; a garment is dipped in kid's blood, and a pledge is taken by Tamar for a kid; Tamar's successful seduction is deemed righteous, but Potiphar's wife's attempted seduction is a sin against God.

Earlier I tried to show how many of these themes, especially deception and recognition, go back to Jacob's early struggle with Esau for the blessing and at the same time look forward to Joseph's recognizing his brothers while they were unable to recognize him. Just as Jacob had put kidskins on his arms and neck to deceive Isaac and as Tamar had changed her garb from widow to harlot to deceive Judah, so Joseph's royal garb, given much attention in the narrative, effectively prevents the brothers from recognizing him.

Another key thematic relationship between Genesis 38 and the Joseph narrative has not been pointed out by other scholars. It is introduced in Judah's interior speech in 38:11. After losing Er and Onan, Judah sends Tamar back to her father's house until his younger son shall grow up. Readers learn instantly what only gradually becomes apparent to Tamar: Judah's action is a ruse to protect the life of his youngest son, "for he thought 'lest he die also like his brothers.' "* Marriage to Tamar seemed to invite death. Chapter 38 proceeds to describe the desperate risk that Tamar takes so that she may bear a child—and the family of Judah will continue. She deceives the deceiver. Tamar becomes pregnant by Judah; and when the patriarch recognizes the pledge tokens and realizes the meaning of her action, he says, "She is more righteous than I, because I did not give her to Shelah, my son."* Thus we see Judah's growth in Genesis 38 as he moves from an understandable desire to protect his youngest son, given in interior speech, to a public proclamation of his wrong. The episode ends with a description of Judah's line continuing—not through Shelah, who remains outside this story—but through the twin offspring of Tamar.

As Seybold has pointed out, Onan's selfish refusal to continue the family of his dead brother through Tamar establishes a thematic parallel with the action of the brothers in Genesis 37, who become callous wasters of life through their hatred of Joseph. The real point of Genesis 38, however, is that Judah is at first also a waster. Ironically he becomes a waster by trying to safeguard the life of Shelah, his youngest son.

By now it should be clear why it is Judah who can step forward to convince Jacob to send Benjamin. We have noted that Jacob has changed from the bold initiator of chapter 42 who saves his family from famine to the pathetic pleader in chapter 43, shriveled into paralysis because he has put Benjamin's safety above all other considerations. In chapter 38 Judah learned the crucial importance of the continuation of the family. He is able to bring Jacob back to his senses by demonstrating that his protective favoritism for Benjamin will destroy the future generation of the family of Israel. Judah demonstrates to Jacob that Israel must live into the future. Whereas he left personal items in pledge ('rbn) to Tamar until the kid be brought, he now pledges himself (*'rbn*) to Jacob until Benjamin be returned home safely. If not, says Judah, he (not his sons, the next generation) will bear the guilt all his days. That is, Judah is now willing to risk giving up the first-born/favored status he's schemed to win in chapter 37.

After the divining-cup incident Judah again emerges as the brothers' spokesman before the Egyptian lord. Whereas Reuben turned against his brothers and proclaimed his innocence in a similar setting (42:22), Judah admits to Joseph that God has "found out the guilt of your servants" just as surely as the cup had been "found" in Benjamin's sack.

Judah's speech before the Egyptian lord also takes a different direction from his speech to Jacob. Whereas he stressed the preservation and continuation of the family in confronting his father, Judah now focuses on the preservation of the father in addressing the Egyptian lord. As he summarizes the past (once more tying past crime to present predicament), Judah highlights the old man's fragility, his total attachment to the one remaining son of Rachel, and the threat that if harm befall Benjamin the brothers will "bring down . . . my father, mourning, to Sheol."* Whereas he had told Jacob that not risking the life of the son will be the death of Israel as a continuing family, Judah now tells the supposed Egyptian that the life of the father is bound to the life of the youngest son, and that the loss of Benjamin will be the death of Israel, the family's progenitor. True, Judah is himself the pledge for Benjamin's safety, but his speech shows that his father's life is more important to him. Thus he offers to remain in Egypt as slave so that Benjamin may go up with his brothers and so that Israel may live.

Joseph's dreams were partially interpreted by his brothers and father in chapter 37, but not until Judah's speech are we (and Joseph) given sufficient narrative perspective to reach a more complete interpretation. Judah's speech shows what the brothers have learned—that the loss of a brother would be the death of Jacob-Israel. Perhaps Joseph did not realize what additional grief to his father his test of the brothers would cause. Paradoxically, there is something more important that *Joseph* must learn from *Judah:* the risking/offering up/suffering/descent of a brother can mean life for the family of Israel.

Judah twice alludes to the Sheol descent motif in his speech before Joseph. As Seybold and others have pointed out, the pattern of the opening chapters of the Joseph story is a threefold descent: into the pit, into Egypt, and into prison. Both in the narrative structure and in the mind of Joseph, the hero who had dreamed of dominion was descending. The brothers see Joseph coming and ambiguously refer to him as "ba'al of the dreams." This means something like "hot shot dreamer"; but the allusion to Baal—the Canaanite vegetation god who annually descends into the pit and then arises—underscores the mythic descent pattern of the hero. This pattern is further underlined by Jacob's outburst upon learning of Joseph's death: "I will go down [*yrd*] unto my son, mourning, to Sheol"* (37:35). Meanwhile, we learn, Joseph was "brought down" (*yrd*) to Egypt (39:1). In 40:15 Joseph comments to the butler and banker on his innocent suffering, designating the prison in which he remains as "the pit"—a term synonymous with Sheol in biblical tradition and used only one other time in the Hebrew Bible for a prison.

When Judah offers to remain enslaved in Egypt so that Israel will not enter Sheol and "the lad might go up with his brothers," Joseph is finally able to perceive the full meaning of his life. In chapter 45 he correlates his dreams of ascendancy with his past suffering: "You sold me here [descent] . . . but God . . . has made me a father to Pharaoh [ascendancy]" (45:5, 8). And the purpose of it all, Joseph now sees, is "God *sent* me before you to *preserve life* . . . to *keep alive* for you numerous survivors"* (45:5, 7).

Judah did not realize that, in offering to remain enslaved so that Benjamin could return, he was helping this strange Egyptian understand the meaning of his own life. In fact, however, Joseph was learning the same lesson that Judah had taught Jacob. The narrator underscores this by developing the symmetry between what Joseph claims that God has done with him and what Judah had earlier insisted that Jacob must do with Benjamin: "*Send* the lad with me . . . that we may *live* and not die . . . also our offspring."* That is, the favored one must descend/be offered up/be risked so that "Israel" (referring both to the father and to the clan) might not perish.

Joseph's speech before his brothers in chapter 45 suggests analogies with Abraham, Judah, Jacob, and God in the Genesis story: what Abraham had done willingly with Isaac, what Judah could not do with Shelah, and what Jacob had done grudgingly with Benjamin, God did with Joseph. As the brothers learn that the divine favoritism they had once hated involved the risking/descent of the chosen one so that Israel might live, they can now perceive Joseph's dreams of ascendancy in a new light. But reconciliation among the brothers—a major theme in the Genesis tradition—can begin only as the brothers realize that they have passed the test. They have affirmed their solidarity with Benjamin by returning with him to Joseph's city. And one of their number has gone even further, offering up not his son but himself so that Israel would not enter Sheol and "the lad might go up with his brothers."

Joseph's self-revelation to his brothers in chapter 45 prepares for the larger family reunion involving Jacob that will fulfill Joseph's second dream. The Joseph story has reached its climax and is winding down, but we should remember that it is an episode within the larger story of Jacob. As the second dream unfolds toward its unusual fulfillment, the ancient patriarch again assumes center stage, and the brothers move off to the wings. In the preceding chapters Jacob the heel-grabber had become Jacob the son-grabber—unwilling to risk Benjamin's descent so that the family might live on. When he hears that Joseph is alive, Jacob impulsively determines to go down to see him before dying. The father who once moaned that he would go down, mourning, to Sheol to seek out his dead son Joseph now prepares to go down to Egypt to meet a living ruler. But as he reaches the border, he hesitates, offering "sacrifices to the God of his father Isaac" (46:1). Sheol and Egypt have become analogous in the story. Jacob is about to leave the land of promise, about to enter Egypt. Jacob and the reader must recall earlier episodes involving the ancestors and Egypt in the context of famine: Sarai and Abram go down in 12:10–20 with ambiguous results: was it an act of foolishness or faith? More recently, Isaac was commanded by God not to go down to Egypt when famine again struck the land (26:2ff). Small wonder that Jacob holds back. Is he risking the promise through this descent into Egypt? Will "the God of his father Isaac" sanction this going down?

The descent-ascent motif continues as God addresses Jacob in a night vision. Here the patriarch must appreciate the lesson his sons have learned—he should not fear descent, for "I will go down with you" (46:4). As God's presence prospered Joseph in Potiphar's household and in prison (39:3–5, 21–23), so God's presence will prosper Jacob in his descent, making Israel a thriving nation down in Egypt. "And I will also bring you up again." As God caused Joseph's ascendancy in Egypt, delivering the family and land from famine, so Jacob will be brought up again to Canaan—his body returned amidst the pomp and circumstance of an Egyptian ceremony.

Any reader should now know that the experience of father and son will continue in the descendants: Israel will "go down" as she enters bondage in Egypt. But she also will prosper in her bondage (Exod. 1:5), and finally God will say to Moses: "I have *come down* to deliver [Israel] . . . and to *bring them up* . . . [to] a land flowing with milk and honey" (Exod. 3:8). The belly of Sheol is transformed into a nurturing womb. Although evil was feared or intended at every stage, God has intended it for good (cf. Gen. 50:20).

The second dream is nearing fulfillment. In Gen. 46:29, as father and lost son finally meet, the text says "and he [Joseph] *appeared* unto him (Jacob)"*—using a Hebrew word that consistently describes a theophany in the Bible. The narrator metaphorically suggests Joseph's royal splendor, but the reader is also asked to remember the cosmic dreams of the sun, moon, and stars. After Joseph has settled the family in Goshen, Jacob prepares for death. His primary concern is that he be buried in Canaan. When Joseph vows that he will carry out the proper burial, Jacob "bowed down [*vayyištaḥû*] on the head of the bed"* (47:31). The dream has been fulfilled in its own way, with the object of the verb left ambiguously unstated. When Joseph agrees to be the agent through whom the divine promises made to Jacob in 46:4 are to be carried out, the patriarch "bows down"—in gratitude to the son, but, more important, acknowledging and accepting the mysterious arrangements of providence.

In the following episode, with Jacob hovering near death, Joseph brings his Egyptian-born sons for a blessing and possibly for adoption. Surprisingly, Jacob states that Ephraim and Manasseh are "as Reuben and Simeon." That is, Joseph's offspring are to assume the role of first-born in Israel. Paternal choice and special roles continue. The narrator stresses Jacob-Israel's dim vision "so that he could not see" (48:10). But, says the patriarch, "God has caused me to see your seed"* (48:11). Jacob-Israel will see not as man sees, but as God causes to see.

Jacob continues the motif of divine favoritism—of Ephraim, the younger, over Manasseh. Joseph protests, but Jacob answers "I know, my son, I know" (48:19). We remember the blind Isaac, who gave the blessing to the right son, though unwittingly. Unlike his father, Jacob sees truly. God has shown him through his experience that although brothers may be reconciled, divine favoritism remains. The offspring of Joseph will play out that drama in Israel's future. Through his ordeal with Joseph and Benjamin, and through his final vision of the deity upon leaving Canaan, Jacob has acquired a new perspective. He is now content to accept a mysterious providence that has brought and will continue to bring blessing and tempered reconciliation out of favoritism and conflict. Jacob sees—that his god has firm and knowable purposes that are nevertheless brought to fruition in paradoxical and surprising ways.

Scholars have generally regarded Genesis 49, in which Jacob gives final blessings to his sons, as an example of early Israelite poetry that reflects the political prominence of the tribes of Joseph and Judah in the early monarchical period. Others see the blessing of Judah as eschatological-messianic, pointing to a distant age beyond the time of the writer. It has rarely been noted how well the song dovetails into the larger story of Jacob, with *Leitwörter* and motifs that link the song to earlier episodes in his life. Now at the point of death, Jacob assumes an almost omniscient point of view, as he sees the future emerging from the past. At no point is the playful wonder of his retrospective vision into the future more evident than here: "it started out or looked like X, but lo, it became Y" is a recurring motif. Reuben—the first of Jacob's procreative strength—is no longer first because he "went up" to his father's bed in a premature attempt to assume the rights of primogeniture and the role of the father (cf. 35:22). Simeon and Levi are strong in anger, with implements of violence (their "cutters/cutting" perhaps punning on the cutting of covenant by cutting of foreskins in 34:13–31) that resulted in the slaying of Shechem and Hamor (the man and the ox of 49:6?) with the "edge of the sword." Like the people of Babel who were scattered (*pûṣ*) for building a city, Simeon and Levi will be scattered (*pûṣ*) for conquering Shechem.

We have seen that Judah is a main character in the Joseph story, and that he and Joseph are the two people whose development is most clearly documented. Judah played a leading role in selling his brother into bondage; yet he becomes the key to a positive resolution of the plot. He convinces Jacob to send Benjamin to Egypt and then helps Joseph understand the meaning of his dreams when he describes Jacob's distress and offers to remain in Egypt in Benjamin's stead. I have tried to argue that the incident that changed Judah's perspective was his encounter with Tamar in chapter 38. It is possible that, in his last words on Judah, Jacob is playfully pondering a son's foibles that led to blessing?

Many of Jacob's final blessings in chapter 49 contain words that play on the names of the sons. In the case of his fourth-born, "Judah" (*y'hûdâ*) is closely followed by "praise you" (*yôdûkā*) and "your hand" (*yād*ᵉ*kā*). The end result, for Judah, will be domination over his enemies, with his brothers *bowing down* before him—precisely the role he may have been aiming at by getting rid of Joseph.

"From the prey [*teref*], my son, you have gone up." Are we being invited to compare and contrast Reuben's "going up" to his father's couch with Judah's "going up" from "the prey"? In 37:33 Jacob had exclaimed, upon seeing Joseph's bloody garment: *ṭārōf ṭōraf yôsēf* ("Joseph has surely become a prey"*). Jacob had assumed it was a wild beast that had killed his son, and in Genesis 49 he refers to Judah as a lion's whelp that had gone up from the prey. Is the father identifying the guilty son? A further ambiguity appears when Jacob says, "From the prey, *my son*, you have gone up." Is he referring to Joseph or to Judah when he says "my son"?

Jacob shifts from the image of the brothers bowing before Judah to Judah as a bowing/couching, stretched-out lion. The first term can have a sexual connotation, especially when reinforced in the first half of verse 10 by the reference to the ruler's staff "between his feet" (a sexual euphemism). In this sexual context when Jacob speaks of the "staff not departing from Judah," we are reminded of Judah's sexual encounter with Tamar in which he left his staff with the woman in pledge of payment.

Judah had met Tamar on the road to Timnah, which is located in the valley of Sorek ("vineyard"). This may be the reason that the poet shifts to vineyard imagery (*gefen/śōrēkâ*). Judah had tarried, binding his ass to the vine (49:11). The two words for "ass" (*'ir/*ᵃ*tōn*) may recall the names of Judah's oldest sons *'er* and *'ōnān*. Vines will break; they are not strong enough to hold a tethered ass. The actions and fate of Judah, Er, and Onan threatened the life of the family vine. Whereas Judah earlier participated in the deception of his father by dipping Joseph's cloak in kid's blood, he must now wash his own garments in the blood of the grape flowing from the broken stock, as he experiences the death of Er and Onan.

While smiling grimly over his son's shady past, perhaps seeing analogies to his own youthful days, Jacob ponders its relationship to Judah's blessed future. The son who had schemed mightily to assume the role of the first-born and had then been willing to give it all up in Egypt will indeed have his brothers bow down before him in days to come. The son who had let his staff depart from him — given to Tamar because he had been unwilling to send Sheleh to her — will indeed not lose his staff/scepter of rule again "until Shiloh [Shelah?] comes."* Judah's folly had resulted in the near breaking of the family vine, as Joseph was sold into Egypt, as Er and Onan both perished. Tamar turned the tables, however; and the end result of the rule of Judah's line will be a paradisiacal abundance with grapes and milk in such great supply that clothes can be washed, wine can be drunk, and asses can be tethered without concern for the waste of broken vines.

In most cultures of the ancient Near East, cosmic unity and stability could not be assumed. The world order reflected an ongoing conflict between deities whose power and mood were in constant flux. There was an ever-present threat that the precarious order of creation could slip back into the chaos whence it had come. The primary goal of each culture's myth and ritual was to reestablish and preserve the cosmic order. In later times the pre-Socratics, while scorning mythology, would attempt to reach the same goal through philosophical constructs. Although Israel had her origins among the peoples of the ancient Near East, she reached a different world view at a relatively early stage of her history. The deity who spoke to Moses and the patriarchs could not be fully fathomed, but a unified, stable order underlying the cosmos could be assumed. Israel's covenant ritual affirmed and celebrated the new order that had been manifested in her early history.

Writing of the "revolution of consciousness" sparked by monotheism, Robert Alter describes the effect that the Israelite world view had on biblical narrative. He aptly suggests "prose fiction" as the most appropriate category for understanding biblical narrative, calling it a "mode of knowledge" and "form of play" that gives the writer freedom to explore, shape, and order the close-up nuances and panoramic vistas of human experience. A unified cosmos is presupposed, liberating the writer to focus on the foibles and often mundane quality of human activity. The narrator assumes an omniscient voice, but the reader receives only fleeting glimpses of perfect knowledge.

In concurring with Alter, I am not denying the presence of tribal etiologies, Egyptian background, or conflated sources in the Joseph story. I am maintaining, however, that all these elements have been subsumed in a powerful work of imagination that depicts human beings deciding and acting, both foolishly and wisely, in a world where mortals shape their destiny within a divine plan. The story's conclusion was not predetermined. Dreams may envision what is divinely determined, but they do not delineate the appropriate human response. Joseph could have rejected his brothers when he first saw them in Egypt; Jacob could have refused to send Benjamin; Judah could have allowed Benjamin to remain enslaved in Egypt. The characters brought the story to its fitting conclusion. But the narrator makes it clear that the characters were able to learn and grow only because they were placed in a cosmos that, given proper cooperation from its supporting cast, brings life out of death and transforms evil into good.

The Wooing of Rebekah

Meir Sternberg

> "Men work together," I told him from the heart,
> "Whether they work together or apart."
> ROBERT FROST, "The Tuft of Flowers"

POINT OF VIEW AND ITS BIBLICAL CONFIGURATION

The Bible teaches more than one general lesson about narration. Far from a technical choice, point of view has emerged as an ideological crux and force, none the less artful for being thus engaged. And far from a matter of who speaks or sees what, I shall now proceed to argue, it always forms a combination of perspectives — such as the divine, the quasi-divine or narratorial, and the human views of Saul's anointment or Pharaoh's affliction. Curiously, some theoretical approaches to point of view are akin to biblical geneticism in fragmenting the text into bits of discourse and seeking to assign each to its appropriate originator. That the object is to identify the internal rather than the historical sources of transmission only renders this exercise in atomism all the more ill-judged; and its pursuit among so-called structuralists flies in the face of the very notion of structure as a network of relations.

For one thing, whatever else point of view may be or do, it entails a relation between subject and object, perceiving mind and perceived reality. In this sense, all speakers (or viewers) figure as interpreters, their speech deriving from a process of interpretation and reflecting or betraying an interpretive construct that they would regard as the world and others might dismiss as a lie or illusion. Discourse renders a world from a certain viewpoint. The whole text accordingly

From *The Poetics of Biblical Narrative: Ideological Literature and the Drama of Reading.* © 1985 by Meir Sternberg. Indiana University Press, 1985.

unfolds as a threefold complex—with the most variable interplay between discourse, world, and perspective—whose disentanglement by the reader forms neither a luxury nor a technicality but the very condition of making sense. Who stands behind this piece of language and what does it project? From what viewpoint does that action or description unfold, and why? Can the perceiver be identified and evaluated by the field of perception? Where does the subject end and the object begin? Is this particular reflector ironic or ironized, reliable or biased or even mendacious, or in short, how does his interpretation stand to the text's and ours? These are among the typical questions arising throughout.

Nor is any of the questions resolvable out of context. As well as interacting with all other components, point of view itself forms a system of perspectival relations—one constant, most variable, all mutually defining. Briefly, as I argued elsewhere, narrative communication involves no fewer than four basic perspectives: the author who fashions the story, the narrator who tells it, the audience or reader who receives it, and the characters who enact it. Where the narrator is practically identical with the author, as in Homer or Fielding or indeed the Bible, the discourse therefore operates with three basic relationships that constitute the point of view: between narrator and characters, narrator and reader, reader and characters. Of these relationships, the first alone normally remains constant in its inequality, opposing the omniscient and reliable narrator to his essentially fallible agents. Whereas the two others are amenable to free variation: what the reader knows and how well he judges, for instance, depend on the narrator's strategy of telling. Whether or not he takes us into his confidence will make an enormous difference to the reading, including our ability to identify or discriminate the perspectives of the dramatized observers and correct their subjective distortions of the implied world and world view. But regardless of narrative strategy, if we are to make any sense of the text—to distinguish one refracting medium from another, opinion from fact, shadow from substance, commitment from irony—we must perform these reconstructive operations as best we can. And we can only perform them by making inferences about the different perspectives in relation to one another and above all to the supreme authority that figures as the contextual measure of their validity. A judgment cannot be located along a scale of reliability, nor a description pronounced objective or subjective, nor a character stamped as ignorant or knowing, nor a reading follow an ironic or straight line—except by reference to the contextual norm embodied in the all-authoritative narrator. Which is to say that a text cannot even be decomposed into its perspectival parts without having been recomposed into a coherent whole, an orchestration of voices and a hierarchy of interpretations.

Given these universals of structure and reading, the marks distinguishing each narrative lie in its treatment of the variable factors and relationships. And here the biblical configuration of point of view has quite a few claims to originality. Most notable is its knocking down of the usually impassable barriers separating authoritative teller from fallible characters to admit God to the position of superperceiver as well as superagent. The reasons having already been discussed, we may now focus on the consequences for the overall art of perspective.

Again, the usual theoretical models and taxonomies fail to apply here. For, as with every structure worthy of the name, the displacement of a part launches a chain reaction that transforms the whole set of relations characterizing omniscient narrative. Where the general model of omniscience in literature dispenses with one of the basic perspectives by virtually equating the author with the narrator, the Bible's introduces a new perspective by dissociating God from the characters and aligning him with the narrator. (Within an inspirational framework, God himself even becomes the author of the book as well as of its plot, without forfeiting his agentlike status.) In so doing, as if to complicate matters further and sharpen the peculiarity of the maneuver, the narrative undermines the normal correlation between a viewpoint's mode of existence (within or without the world) and level of authority (nonprivileged or privileged, respectively). Like all commonsensical linkages, this norm may hold in the Bible for the godlike narrator (detached and privileged) as well as for the earthly cast (involved and nonprivileged) but, what is ideologically appropriate, not for divinity itself.

The lines of demarcation are thus redrawn to establish a novel fourfold pattern, involving two assorted and roughly symmetrical couples: the elevated superhumans on the one hand and the erring humans on the other. God existentially inside while perspectivally above the world, the reader wedded in some degree to his fellow men: this structure of point of view acts as a constant reminder of their respective positions in the scheme of things. From this unpromising premise, and not so much despite as because of its theological bearing, there also springs an intricate, flexible, and challenging art of perspective, to which the Wooing of Rebekah in Genesis 24 affords a good introduction.

THE WOOING

Positions and Discrepancies Established

> (1) Abraham was old, advanced in years; and the Lord had blessed Abraham in everything. (2) And Abraham said to his servant, the oldest of his house, who ruled over everything that he had, Put thy hand, pray, under my thigh, (3) and I will make thee swear by the Lord, the God of heaven and the God of the earth, that thou shalt not take a wife for my son from the daughters of the Canaanites,

among whom I dwell; (4) but to my native land [*el artsi ve'el moladeti*] shalt thou go and take a wife for my son, for Isaac. (5) And the servant said to him, Perhaps the woman may not be willing to follow me to this land; shall I then lead thy son back to the land from which thou camest? (6) And Abraham said to him, Take care that thou dost not lead my son back there. (7) The Lord, the God of heaven, who took me from my father's house and from the land of my birth [*erets moladeti*], and who spoke to me and swore to me, saying, To thy offspring will I give this land, he will send his angel before thee and thou shalt take a wife for my son from there. (8) And if the woman is not willing to follow thee, then thou wilt be free of this oath of mine; only thou shalt not lead my son back there. (9) So the servant put his hand under the thigh of Abraham his master and swore to him concerning this matter.

This is a scene to which the reader has been looking forward for some time, and not merely because the original audience must have known, as every schoolboy now does, that Isaac married Rebekah. The accidentals of the extratextual knowledge brought to the reading are standardized by the internal knowledge built into the reading process. And since narrative tact as well as poetics rules out the baldness of an overt foreshadowing, this internalization takes a form subtle enough to keep even the knowledgeable reader occupied, yet determinate enough to enlighten the less informed.

It is the analogy between Abraham's two sons that first anticipates the marital theme. Ishmael's career shows three landmarks: late birth (Gen. 16:16), mortal danger averted by a timely divine intervention (21:14–19), and marriage to a compatriot of his Egyptian mother's (21:21). Isaac having likewise gone through the first two stages (21:1–8; 22:1–12), the third is now due by compositional logic. That expectation even gains further point from the tightening of the analogy toward the final stage. The divine promise "I will make him a great nation" (21:18), which came between Ishmael's ordeal and his marriage, now recurs with redoubled force after the sacrificial binding of Isaac: "I will indeed bless thee and I will multiply thy offspring as the stars of heaven and the sand on the seashore, and thy offspring shall possess the gate of his enemies" (22:17). The fulfillment of this promise—significantly echoed at both the beginning (24:7) and the end (24:60) of our tale—again requires a bride. And indeed, as if on cue, she or at least her name makes an immediate entrance:

After these things, it was told to Abraham, Behold, Milcah too has borne sons, to Nahor thy brother: Uz his firstborn, Buz his brother, Kemuel the father of Aram, Kesed, Hazo, Pildash, Yidlaf, and Bethuel.

And Bethuel begot Rebekah. These eight Milcah bore to Nahor, Abraham's brother. And his concubine, whose name was Reumah, also bore Tebah, Tahash, and Ma'acah.

(Gen. 22:20–24)

This material could hardly seem less promising: a bare genealogical list of supernumeraries, with none but remote antiquarian value. Yet even catalogues bring grist to the Bible's mill, and the lump of history gets assimilated to the art of the personal story. Inserted under the guise of family news, this digression assumes new shape and meaning in context. The genealogical list falls into analogical pattern, the chronological parataxis ("After these things") stiffens into causal sequence, the retrospect turns round its face to become a prospection. Juxtaposed with God's blessing and placed in structural correspondence to Ishmael's marriage, the report virtually names the bride-to-be. Not, however, in a manner so transparent as to destroy the pleasures of inference. That is why Rebekah gets tucked away in the middle, and a rival candidate, Ma'acah, occupies a far more prominent position. But the camouflage arrests and amuses rather than misleads even the unforewarned reader. Ma'acah is clearly a red herring: a concubine's daughter, in a cycle where mixed descent has played such an unsettling role, she might be a good match for Ishmael but hardly for Abraham's heir. And Rebekah's obtrusive presence amply makes up for her unobtrusive location. In a list supposed to enumerate the "sons" that "Milcah too has borne"—the allusion to Sarah in "too" interprets *banim* as "sons" rather than "children"—why include a female who is not even a daughter? Of Nahor's presumably numerous descendants, moreover, Rebekah is the only grand-daughter mentioned. And as if to italicize the clue, her mention is at once followed by a summative numbering ("These eight Milcah bore to Nahor") that pointedly excludes her. The coherence of that item, the signals imply, must be sought along lines other than genealogical.

The indirections that culminate in this miniature guess-who puzzle, then, serve as a built-in anticipation, elevating the reader to a vantage post from which he identifies Rebekah as the God-appointed bride. But does Abraham, the dramatized recipient of the family news, share this foreknowledge? It is interesting that, where we might expect him to name Rebekah, he does not even direct his servant to her family. This strange failure has often been missed, due to the common fallacy of hindsight reading and specifically a misreading of verse 4. The point needs to be established, therefore, as the groundwork of the tale's play of viewpoints and its overall sense.

It is a fact that the faithful servant does not at all approach the family on arrival, but stops at the well to contrive a test that opens the field to every girl in the town. Indeed, he does not depart for Nahor's house in the first place: his destination is given rather as "Mesopotamia, the city of Nahor." (This reference need not even be to a person but to the place that figures as Nakhur in the Mari tablets.) And the servant's proceeding not only reflects but follows his instructions. Note that Abraham, far from pronouncing the name that is trembling on *our* lips, starts with a general characterization of the bride required and a negative characterization at that: "not from the daughters of the Canaanites, among whom I dwell." And as the dialogue begins so does it proceed and end—with the negative feature of Canaan looming larger than any positive attraction of Mesopotamia, let alone any specific Mesopotamian. Hence the harping on the spatial opposition between "here" and "there" that depersonalizes the whole transaction. In case the woman refuses to settle in "this land," the servant asks, shall Isaac join her "in the land from which thou camest?" No, Abraham insists, he must not return "there": God, who promised my offspring "this land," will see to it that you bring a woman "from there." Yet whatever happens, there is no question of Isaac's settling "there." Which clearly means that, destined to inherit the land, Isaac must on no account marry among those doomed to disinheritance; but since Mesopotamia's recommendation lies in not being Canaan, it would lose all appeal were Isaac to disinherit himself by emigrating. The historical process launched by Abraham's call must no more be reversed by his son's repatriation than subverted by local intermarriage.

No wonder, therefore, that Abraham frames the scenario in the widest ethno-geographical terms; that he makes no mention of his brother Nahor, perhaps even in a deliberate attempt to bring home his point and minimize the danger of emigration; that he impersonalizes the bride into "a woman." He acts from a sense of national destiny rather than from family feeling or nostalgia for his old country. And the servant, who would otherwise appear a disobedient fool or knave, jeopardizing if not sabotaging his mission by his failure to make a beeline for the family address, simply observes his terms of reference.

Within these terms of reference, accordingly, the direction *el artsi ve'el moladeti telekh* in verse 4 does not bear the meaning "thou shalt go to my land and to my kindred," assigned to it by most translators and exegetes. It rather forms a hendiadys signifying "thou shalt go to the land of my kindred/birth" or "to my native land," precisely like the *erets moladeti* of verse 7. In the context of the Abraham saga, as it happens, *moledet* refers to an entity larger than the family anyway. God's very first address to Abraham, "Go forth from thy land and thy *moledet* and thy father's house to the land that I will show thee" (Gen. 12:1), marks an ascending order of specificity where *moledet* falls between country and kindred. Given the otherwise symmetrical relations between the divinely ordered exodus ("go forth from . . . ") and the humanly ordered return ("go to . . . "), moreover, Abraham's omission of the specific "father's house" from the reversed scenario would make little sense were it not for its perfect congruity with the impersonal spirit of the "here-there" opposition. In retrospect, indeed, we note that when the servant rewrites history to cajole the relatives into believing that Abraham expressly directed him to them, he thrice replaces in transmission Abraham's original "land and *moledet*" by "father's house and family" (Gen. 24:38, 40, and 41). The version revised after the event to narrow down the field only highlights the generality of the original intention.

By the time the servant puts his hand under his master's thigh, therefore, the tale has already established a fourfold (and practically, threefold) structure of point of view, with marked and gradated discrepancies in awareness. God (who promised) and the narrator (who anticipated the fulfillment) stand together at one pole, their supernatural knowledge going with absolute control. The opposite pole is occupied by the patriarch and his envoy, their powers so humanly limited that they can no more foresee than ensure the outcome: to them the issue remains open against their desire, its concrete terms to be disclosed only in historical embodiment, its resolution problematic and fraught with danger. In between stands the reader, privileged enough to foreknow the end as determinate and happy even beyond the characters' dreams, but reduced to ignorance in all that concerns the route leading up to the providential end.

This conforms to the Bible's favorite system of perspectival relations, serving to reconcile the claims of art and ideology into a happy ideological art. God, omniscient and omnipotent by doctrinal fiat, will prove so in dramatic terms as the action translates his implicit will and pledge into the stuff of history: the premise lays the ground for the demonstration and the demonstration vindicates and inculcates the premise—which sounds poor logic but makes excellent rhetoric in the telling. At the same time as the narrator exploits his authority to dramatize and glorify God's, God's own powers invest the compositional foreshadowing-by-analogy with such force as to enable the narrator to canalize interest into the desired grooves without compromising his art of indirection. In turn, the characters' limited knowledge, governed by the realistic norm, first establishes a sharp opposition between the natural and the supernatural spheres and then motivates a progressive discovery of God's benevolent control. The reader's intermediate position, finally, guarantees his awareness of God's superintendence, while leaving the movement from promise to fulfillment dark enough to sustain interest and allow the demonstration to work itself out in human terms. Given the initial sense of divine providence, the interplay of character and event may develop with impunity.

Typical in essentials, this perspectival scheme yet manifests some variables. Above all, the Bible does not often effect such a severance between the informational and the normative axes of point of view. Considered by themselves, the informational tensions might be expected to generate powerful irony at the expense of the least knowing, the dramatis personae. But we actually experience little irony, because the discrepancies in awareness are tempered by parity in values: knowledge of principles always redeems in the Bible any lacunae in the knowledge of facts and contingencies; though not, as evildoers find out the hard way, vice versa. Thus, the implied reader shares—if only by artful courtesy—the narrator's world view. But so does Abraham, who, ignorant of all details and personalities, is still confident that God "will send his angel" to look after them. And so, it progressively emerges, does his servant, who speaks and acts for him throughout as a like-minded ambassador. As he sets out, therefore, the variations between the nondivine perspectives yet go with the question common to all fellow-believers: *How* will God manage the affair?

The Movement from Divergence to Convergence of Perspectives

(10) The servant took ten camels of the camels of his master and went, with all kinds of goods from his master in his hand; and he arose and went to Mesopotamia, to the city of Nahor. (11) And he made the camels kneel down outside the city by the well of water at evening time, the time when the women come out to draw water. (12) And he said, O Lord, God of my master Abraham, make things go well for me this day and show kindness to my master Abraham. (13) Behold, I am standing by the spring of water, and the daughters of the men of the city are coming out to draw water. (14) The maiden to whom I shall say, Pray let down thy pitcher that I may drink, and who will say, Drink, and I shall water thy camels too—let her be the one whom thou hast appointed for thy servant Isaac. (15) Before he had finished speaking, and behold, Rebekah came out, who was born to Bethuel the son of Milcah, the wife of Nahor, Abraham's brother, with her pitcher upon her shoulder. (16) And the maiden was very good-looking, a virgin, and no man had known her. She went down to the spring and filled her pitcher and came up. (17) And the servant ran towards her and said, Pray give me a little water to drink from thy pitcher. (18) And she said, Drink, my lord; and she made haste and lowered her pitcher onto her hand and let him drink. (19) And when she had finished letting him drink, she said, I shall draw for thy camels too, until they have finished drinking. (20) And she made haste and emptied her pitcher into the trough, and ran again to the well to draw, and she drew for all his camels. (21) And the man stood wondering at her, keeping silent to learn whether the

Lord had prospered his journey or not. (22) And when the camels had finished drinking, the man took a gold ring, half a shekel in weight, and two bracelets for her hands, ten gold shekels in weight. (23) And he said, Whose daughter art thou? Pray tell me. Is there room in thy father's house for us to spend the night? (24) And she said to him, I am the daughter of Bethuel the son of Milcah, whom she bore to Nahor. (25) And she said to him, We have both straw and provender in plenty, also room to spend the night in. (26) And the man bowed his head and worshipped the Lord. (27) And he said, Blessed be the Lord, the God of my master Abraham, who has not withheld his kindness and his truth from my master. I being on a journey, the Lord has led me to the house of my master's brothers.

Thrown on his own devices on arrival, the servant leaves nothing to chance, as his mandate entitled him to do, but takes a twofold initiative that weds good sense to piety. Of the eligible young women in the city, he will not settle for less than the best. So, appealing to God to bless his principle of choice, he improvises a shrewd character test. What touchstone could be more appropriate than the reception of a wayfarer to determine a woman's fitness to marry into the family of the paragon of hospitality? And it is a stiff test, too, since it would require far more than common civility to volunteer to water "ten" thirsty camels. (Note how this initially descriptive, realistic-looking feature now gains actional and thematic value as well: from a measure of Abraham's wealth, it transforms into a measure of his daughter-in-law's worthiness to enjoy it.)

The perfection of the initiative thus continues to moderate the irony threatened by the discrepancies in foreknowledge. Yet these discrepancies make for variance even in the application of the perfect yardstick. What to the servant is a character test of a prospective bride is to the reader a retrospective (and exhilarating) characterization of Rebekah. Having already been cast in the bridal role, how can she fail to pass with flying colors?

Indeed, her entrance could hardly be more auspicious. Where a folktale would first stage two or three abortive trials, in the interests of variety and retardation and contrastive portrayal, the Bible brings on the appointed winner at once. Not that it spurns the effects yielded by a drawn-out process—we shall see them all generated by oblique means. Rather, the narrative's primary concern is to show God at his invisible work, and any serialization of the test would upset the balance between human ingenuity and divine control. Far from delayed, therefore, the girl shows up even "before he had finished speaking." She is, literally, God's answer (in the medium of plot) to the servant's prayer; and so in fact do both he and we view her. However, we reach that conclusion with much greater certitude, thanks to a sudden widening of the informational discrepancy to our advantage. Though the new development seems to emerge from the servant's viewpoint ("and behold!"), the narrator smuggles into the report three facts inaccessible to any human observer. It is by his privilege and for our benefit alone that the text reveals the water-drawer's name ("Rebekah"), her lineage ("born to Bethuel," etc., to jog the memory of forgetful readers), and, most hidden and reassuring, her morals ("a virgin," etc.). Less favored, the dramatized spectator is also less reassured. The timing is perfect, the good looks a welcome bonus, but what about the character? Only the test can show.

The test does, of course, show. But it performs this role beyond anyone's expectations and with a consummate art that has been mistaken by hardline geneticists for patchwork and by their modern heirs for "an original narrative prolixity . . . made wordier still by subsequent transmission," with the extenuating circumstance that "the repetitiveness which we occasionally find a bit over-whelming was not so sensed by the authors and editors of the Bible." It is only by the grace of what I called the Bible's foolproof composition that such extreme under-readers yet manage to grasp the essentials of plot and judgment, without suffering anything worse than boredom. If "we" find anything overwhelming, it is not at all the repetitiveness but the fireworks of repetition.

The variations in the passage from wish to fulfillment have a random look, since they manifest the wildest heterogeneity: changes in wording, in continuity, in specification. Below the surface, however, all this formal variety combines into functional unity. All the variations go to dramatize a single point: that the young woman's performance surpasses even the most optimistic expectations. Thus, the increased specificity largely derives from the references to haste that punctuate the narrative: "she made haste and lowered her pitcher . . . she made haste and lowered her pitcher into the trough . . . she ran again to the well." This spontaneous dispatch bears more than the obvious complimentary implica-tions for character and judgment. It echoes nothing less than Abraham's model hospitality, "He ran to meet them . . . Abraham made haste into the tent . . . Abraham ran to the tent . . . he made haste to prepare it" (Gen. 18:2–7); and the elevating analogy stamps her as worthy of the patriarch himself. Hence also another rise in particularity, from the envisaged "drawing" of water to its actual enactment, "she went down to the spring and filled her pitcher and came up." This meticulous picture of the girl descending empty and then ascending loaded suggests what an arduous chore the drawing of water is, literally uphill work, even in normal conditions; how exhausting when one goes down and up at a run; how interminable when one has to provide for a whole caravan; and all (another recurrent detail) with one little pitcher.

The watering must have taken quite a while; and this is further stressed in Gen. 24:21 by the description of the man as "wondering at her, keeping silent to learn whether the Lord had prospered his journey or not," otherwise oddly interpolated between two mentions of her performance. In temporal terms, this discontinuous repetition marks a sequence of "action → regression → progression," and in terms of point of view, a shift from our perspective to the servant's. The reader, who knows that the maiden is destined to complete the service she has undertaken, needs no special telling that "she drew for all his camels." But while she is breaking her back for him, the internal observer can hardly believe what she has already done and only hope ("or not" is for him still on the cards) that she will get through with her task. The descriptive realism, in short, renders the well scene anything but an idyllic encounter: the emphasis rather falls on the correlation between the volunteer's physical labor and moral worth.

That she does more than could be expected becomes doubly impressive in view of the fact that he asks for less. The envisioned request "Pray lower thy pitcher that I may drink" drops to "Pray give me a little water to drink from thy pitcher." So it is she who prolongs the sip into a full-sized drink, just as she thinks of supporting the pitcher for the drinker's convenience and adds the deferential "my lord" in addressing what is to the narrator "the servant" or at most "the man." As for the camels, everyone hopes of course that she will offer to "water" them, but the scope of her initiative again surprises the covert as well as the dramatized observer: "For thy camels too I will draw, *until they have finished drinking*." And however formidable the undertaking, she means exactly what she says, as the narrator underlines through another subtle (in Hebrew, even punning) repetition with variation. "She drew for *all* his camels" (*kol,* full number) and "the camels *finished* drinking" (*killu,* full belly).

Only at one point, the very outset, does the variation in performance give real cause for concern. Where expected to respond "Drink and I shall water thy camels too," she actually stops halfway through: "Drink, my lord." Even the stoutest heart will miss a beat at this. Is she the type that will oblige at request but offer nothing beyond? Does she overlook the camels thoughtlessly or deliberately? Is it one thing to "lower" a pitcher for a single man and quite another to exhaust oneself on behalf of his thirsty beasts? Owing to the discrepancies in information, these gaps must have troubled the servant even more than the reader: our perplexity about Rebekah may well have been his despair of the first candidate. He may already have written her off when, upon the girl's delivering the second part as well, and to more than perfection, it all turns out to be a false alarm.

In retrospect we discover that the narrator has mixed a little mischief with serious business to extraordinary effect. The mischief consists in retarding the plot with a view to heightened suspense. But the retardation is more cunning and multifunctional than it looks. In playing on our fears, it also serves to insinuate by the backstairs of composition the abortive trial that a folktale would introduce by the front door of the action. Due to our initial ignorance of her personality, Rebekah assumes for a moment the features and fate of a heroine who, if not an utter washout, does not come up to matriarchal standard. Her unfolding thus spread or distributed over two stages, she functions as a two-in-one. Rebekah-of-the-first-half ("Drink, my lord") enriches the plot by indirection and makes the real Rebekah shine by contrast. Far from gratuitous, still less detrimental, the false alarm proves salutary: this is often the case with the piecemeal and tortuous emergence of literary character, and Rebekah affords us the first example of the Bible's command of this art of (temporary or, elsewhere, permanent) ambiguity. We appreciate her true self all the more for not being allowed to take its virtues for granted.

This contrast-in-sequence is enhanced, moreover, by surprise as well as suspense and relief. Not Rebekah's behavior and character alone but even her motives prove contrary to our initial fears. If she responds by installments, it is only because she will not lump together man and beast. Only after she has "finished letting him drink" does she express her readiness to do the same for the camels. Just as she began by injecting into her speech the deferential "my lord," so does she end by showing more tact than could be foreseen or perhaps even required. What threatened failure reveals itself as another God-sent bonus and blessing. She has certainly earned the costly gifts presented to her on the spot.

That the servant must have shared much of our experience (apprehension, enlightenment, character inference) marks a shift in perspectival design and relations. What we have been tracing amounts to a twofold movement that is integral to the Bible's dynamics of point of view. One movement consists in a process of illumination within each of the limited perspectives — the reader's and the hero's — that brings them closer by degrees to the static pole of the omniscient. At this stage, though still not so privileged as God and the narrator themselves, each of the human observers has gained considerable insight into the disposition of things. Relatively, of course, the servant has made more progress since the outset, but that is in keeping with another feature of the strategy. If the first dynamics consists in a progressive narrowing of informational discrepancies vis-à-vis the omniscient, the second involves a convergence of the restricted viewpoints themselves. Having been launched from different starting points along the scale of knowledge, they are then propelled forward not only in the same direction but also at a pace variable enough to allow the one behind to overtake and keep more or less abreast of the one who got a head start.

The narrative began by conferring on the reader an informational advantage over master and servant, through oblique pointers to Rebekah. Abraham then fades out, and the plot traces the envoy's route to knowledge and success. On arrival, his initiative commands personal admiration and doctrinal assent but, as formerly with the master, it is not at once rewarded with enlightenment. On the contrary, his ignorance relative to the reader deepens owing to the narrator's un-evenhanded treatment of Rebekah's entrance; and the resultant discrepancy leads to further variations in the response to her conduct, dooming the less informed observer to lowered understanding and heightened suspense. The test once under way, however, the two viewpoints begin to converge. Not only do we experience much of his alarm at the threat of failure, but he attains to much of our knowledge when all ends well.

Regarding ignorance and knowledge alike, to be sure, this new alignment is not yet perfect, nor, as a matter of principle, will it ever evolve into strict identity. Apart from all contingencies, it makes an essential difference that, though equally concerned to penetrate appearances and unravel mysteries by way of interpretation, the servant is not a "reader" in the sense that we are. Like all figural interpreters, he directly confronts a world that we receive through the mediation of an artful teller and text. He exercises interpretation on the world of objects; we, on a web of words that projects such a world. And whatever the similarity between these worlds, notably in divine control, each still retains its features and constraints vis-à-vis the interpreter: each, in my earlier formulation, remains a distinct semiotic system, with its own medium, communicator, addressee, and rules of decipherment.

Thus, the servant's knowledge is regulated by God, ours by the narrator, and the two omniscients operate with different means even to the same end. In the absence of explicit foretelling, as here, the reader's foreknowledge and expectations derive from probabilities beyond the agent's ken. The structural anticipations of Rebekah relate far more to the logic (arrangement, coherence, conventions) of the text than of the world; and even if noticed, would hardly carry the same weight for "real life" interpreters as for one facing a verbal artifice. Or consider even the latent parallels between Rebekah's and Abraham's hospitality. The rationale of the test implies that the servant may also have detected them, but only in general outline: since he observes events not words, he could not have been affected by the linguistic echoes of "haste" that clinch the analogy for us. In general . . . the poetics of the narrative is reserved for the reader's viewpoint and interpretive operations.

Moreover, the dramatized interpreter and his interpreting are themselves part of the represented world and accordingly, like everything else, objects of the reader's interpretation. This builds into the pattern an ironic discrepancy in our favor. But the irony can be sharpened ad hoc, as with Samuel the anointer, through the manipulation of specific perspectival disparities; or it can be attenuated and even neutralized ad hoc, through the reduction of such variations to the point of denying the reader any sense of superiority—not at least beyond that inherent in the position of secretly watching and eavesdropping on a character who goes about his business unaware of being made a show of. Hence the significance of our tale's early alignment of the normative viewpoints and, along the informational axis, its movement from initial tensions to relative harmony. Both go a long way toward bridging the distance between the observers with their distinct posts and sources and procedures of observation. In line with this movement, the ensuing dialogue not only brings them closer but also, though holding far more disclosures and surprises for the servant than for the reader, makes a two-level discovery scene, where he recognizes a set of factors and we applaud his recognitions.

Far from being looked down on for his ignorance of the recipient's identity, the ambassador further endears himself to us by covering Rebekah with gold, because it is exactly his unawareness of the fact that clinches his awareness of the principle: the young woman has earned the gifts, since nothing counts like personal merit. The factual discrepancy itself then gets bridged in the dialogue scene. What is more, the girl's speech affords another chance for perspectival convergence in the observation of her exquisite manners, whose finer points would hardly be lost on an Oriental and a great man's steward at that. She answers the questions in the order but, with the same regard for decorum, not always in the terms in which they are posed. "Whose daughter art thou?" receives the straightforward answer, "I am the daughter of Bethuel," where the omission of her own name spares the questioner, at whatever cost to ego, a detail in which he expressed no interest. But to the inquiry about "room in thy father's house for us to spend the night" she diplomatically replies by stating the objective facilities for hospitality, without extending even to a munificent stranger the invitation that is not hers to extend.

No sooner has this model bride crowned her performance than the reader finds his sentiments and reasoning voiced by the servant, who takes none of the credit for himself but puts it all where it is ideologically due. He does the right thing on the right grounds. Since in a God-directed world there is no room for coincidence, the encounter with Abraham's grandniece must be an act of providence. (He has started, we recall, with the believer's shibboleth, "Make things go well for me," or in literal paradox, "devise an accident for me.") This declaration of faith thus crowns the meeting of the reader's early anticipation, formed by appeal to the poetic coherence of the text, and the character's later recognition, anchored in the doctrine of the existential coherence of the world. And since the biblical text itself largely depends for its coherence on the assumption of divine control—the narrator playing providence only in God's name and to

God's glory — the man's simple piety reinforces rather than just parallels our more complex interpretation.

New Tensions and Final Resolution

Among its other roles, the next phase seals this marriage of true minds:

(28) The maiden ran and told her mother's household about these things. (29) Now Rebekah had a brother whose name was Laban; and Laban ran out to the man, to the spring. (30) And on seeing the ring and the bracelets on his sister's hands, and on hearing the words of Rebekah his sister, saying, Thus and so did the man speak to me, he went to the man; and behold, he was standing by the camels at the spring. (31) And he said, Come, O blessed of the Lord; why dost thou stand outside? I have prepared the house, and room for the camels. (32) And the man came into the house, and he ungirded the camels and gave straw and provender for the camels and water to wash his feet and the feet of the men who were with him. (33) Then food was set before him to eat, and he said, I will not eat until I have spoken my piece. And he said, Speak.

In terms of plot structure, this episode clearly performs a bridging function. The second movement of the action having been completed with the discovery of the bride, the logic of causality now requires the servant's arrival at the house to launch the movement that will end in the departure for Canaan with the family's blessing. And since protocol forbids the girl's inviting him herself, the narrator packs her off home to summon a higher authority, embodied in Laban. For a causal link between highlights, however, the episode certainly looks overtreated, unrolling at a leisurely pace and with circumstantial detail associated with the Homeric rather than the biblical style. It looks even more so from the reader's vantage point, since foreknowledge presses for a quick transition to the business at hand. Of course, the lingering heightens our expectancy. Yet judged by the economies of biblical narrative, suspense alone does not justify the extent of the retardation — as noted at the foregoing stage — still less the minutiae that compose it. This sense of excess indicates a search for tighter and less obvious coherence.

The whole passage gains intelligibility from its implications for character and perspective. These not only elaborate but also parallel the overt plot function in that they likewise work backward and forward at the same time, linking antecedents to consequents. Thus, the dispatch with which Rebekah fulfills her plot assignment ("ran" not "went") rounds off her characterization by giving us an insight into her mind: it suggests more than ordinary goodwill to the stranger and lessens the fear that she may refuse to follow him. No sooner have we gathered that the obstacles if any will come from the family, than Laban enters the picture: his immediate role in the plot (as host) motivates his portrayal in anticipation of his ultimate role (as guardian).

That portrayal itself looks back to the young woman's, just as it looks ahead to the negotiation scene. Laban's "running" follows so hard upon Rebekah's as to give him the benefit of all the favorable effects associated with her haste throughout: the whole family, it seems, is a credit to Abraham. No later than the next verse, however, this carry-over impression proves misleading. The initial similarity turns into contrast as the narrator doubles back in time from the hospitable action ("he ran") to its ulterior motive (the sight of "the ring and the bracelets"). And when the action resumes ("he went"), we find the contrast settled through an inside view in free indirect style ("and behold") where "the camels" prominently figure, as indeed they are to do twice again in relation to Laban's solicitude. Accordingly, even his pious address to the stranger as "blessed of the Lord" sounds an ironic note, sharpened by unwitting allusion to God's promise to "bless" Abraham by multiplying his descendants (Gen. 22:17) and to Abraham's being "blessed in everything" (24:1). Ignorant of antecedents and identities, Laban twists this charged phrase into homage to material blessing.

This sequential shift in portrayal repeats the technique through which Rebekah's figure and mind have been unfolded, and insinuates anew the theme of the abortive test. But its point lies in reversing the earlier movement (verses 18–19) from unfavorable to favorable impression. While Laban's initial correspondence to Rebekah somewhat dims her virtues by suggesting a family portrait, the sudden about-face highlights her singularity more than ever before: she shines in contrast to what her analogue actually is as well as to what she herself might have been. And while the initial correspondence bodes good for the servant's endeavors in the coming negotiations, its breakdown-and-reversal intensifies suspense by disclosing the kind of people he has to deal with. The indirect revelation of character through details in excess of plot exigencies thus affects our understanding and expectations of the plot itself.

This new disturbing element, however, consolidates the recent perspectival alliance between reader and ambassador. To start with, our relations with him and with Laban have developed in opposed directions. Laban has our approval as long as he seems to rush out on instinct, but he forfeits it as soon as it transpires that his bustle was prompted by knowledge of the traveler's wealth. The disclosure of informational parity here not only fails to ensure but actively unsettles his normative alignment with the reader: this makes a telling opposition to the process whereby our moral bond with the servant has counteracted (and foretold the decrease in) informational imparity. Principle always outranks fact, whether considered as dimensions of the Bible's epistemology or its structure of point of view. And in providing a negative illustration of this scale, Laban serves to draw us yet closer to the servant as well as to Rebekah.

Again, not that the two viewpoints perfectly coincide. The insight afforded us into Laban's mind is, as privileged *and* compositional disclosure, beyond the servant's reach; just as the opacity of the servant's own mind puts his current thoughts beyond ours. We are still due for some of those surprises that keep biblical man somewhat less — or, aesthetically, more — than a known quantity even on the closest acquaintance. Yet the emergence of a new, threatening viewpoint reinforces our sense of familiarity and solidarity with the old. While the family is still in the dark, moreover, we are privy to the servant's predicament and intentions, share his hopes and to a lesser extent his fears, and, judging from his past performance with its combination of ingenuity and faith, can even hazard an informed guess as to his general tactics. In retrospect, of course, even the remaining gaps and discrepancies vanish. But hindsight is an aid to rather than a condition of our involvement, inference, irony at the expense of the unknowing. Of all listeners, we alone are in a position to appreciate his maneuvers and motives throughout an address where he rarely speaks straight (for expository convenience, I divided the speech into its tactical blocks, but it may be well to read it as a whole first):

> (34) And he said, I am Abraham's servant. (35) The Lord has abundantly blessed my master and he has become great; he has given him sheep and cattle, silver and gold, manservants and maidservants, camels and asses. (36) And Sarah my master's wife bore a son to my master after reaching old age, and he has given him everything he has.

The materialistic exordium shows that the speaker had no need of our privileges to take Laban's measure. The harping on wealth and status begins as early as the formal self-identification, "I am Abraham's servant." For by identifying himself in these self-effacing terms, as though he did not have so much as a name of his own, he at once transfers to his master all the benefits of the impressive entrance: the costly gifts, the ten loaded camels, and "the men who were with him" (their mention reserved for the arrival at the house to suggest the family's viewpoint). It is not he who is "blessed of the Lord," the servant indeed goes on to emphasize in pointed and corrective allusion to Laban's form of address, but Abraham: "The Lord has abundantly blessed my master." So much so, that all they have observed amounts only to a fraction of this blessing. "Sheep and cattle, silver and gold, manservants and maidservants, camels and asses": the items in full view ("gold," "manservants," "camels") are so interspersed as to command belief in their unseen mates; and, against the background of the narrator's shorthand (e.g., 13:2), the range of the catalogue signals the dramatized speaker's reluctance to leave much to his audience's imagination. The opening verse thus marks a steady progression in the inducement of the thought, "If such are his servants, how great must the master be!"

Immediately thereafter, however, the speaker passes to another branch of family news, or so his unforewarned auditors may think. From our vantage point, we easily trace the connection: the next step in the softening-up process is to introduce the prospective bridegroom, display his eligibility, and transfer to him in turn the aura of material blessing. All this gets accomplished without giving the show away. Isaac, the hidden subject of the discourse, comes in only as grammatical object—first of Sarah's "bearing" and then of Abraham's "giving." He even remains nameless, his presence thus subordinated (indeed like Rebekah's on her first appearance amid Nahor's descendants) to the heading of good news about familiar relatives. The audience will be caught all the more effectively if led to believe that they are forming their own conclusions. Hence the sandwiching of the "son" between two otherwise overspecific references to his parents: born by "Sarah the wife of my master" (a reminder of her legal status) to "my master" (harking back to the wealth and establishing legitimacy). Hence also "when she was old, " an indication of time ostensibly meant to provoke cheers for the mother but in fact calculated to recommend the son. If she was old at the time, then he is still young now; and if she bore him by a miracle, then he must be blessed and is certainly the only heir. (No mention of Ishmael, naturally.) Indeed, the bland tempter proceeds, his father has already "given him everything he has." This anticipates matters a bit, since Abraham makes over his property to Isaac (in these very words) only before his death (25:5). But since the present company cannot know, the intention may pass for the deed.

The man's art lies not so much in the slight stretching of the facts as in their thorough insinuation. And to mask his drift, the persuader varies his technique from the first step to the second. Abraham's riches can be safely painted in the most glowing colors, under the cover story of "You will be happy to learn that. . . . " But when it comes to his deficiency of children, that pretext would hardly serve. Therefore the speaker so wraps up the topic as to invite the deduction that the parent's misfortune is the son's good fortune: to let the thought "What a catch!" steal into the audience's mind before they find him actually offered to them on a hard condition.

> (37) And my master made me swear, saying, Thou shalt not take a wife for my son from among the daughters of the Canaanites in whose land I dwell. (38) But to my father's house shalt thou go and to my kindred, and take a wife for my son. (39) And I said to my master, Perhaps the woman will not follow me. (40) And he said

to me, The Lord, before whom I walk, will send his angel with thee and prosper thy journey, and thou shalt take a wife for my son from my kindred and from my father's house. (41) Then shalt thou be clear of my oath, when thou comest to my kindred; and if they will not give thee, thou shalt be clear of my oath.

To the unsuspecting materialist, it would indeed prove a catch with a catch. Since Abraham's condition is too operational to be much watered down, the rhetoric addresses itself to pressing for its acceptance. And having already made the most of the worldly blandishments, it now shifts its focus to the familial. What appeared so far the object of a report becomes the frame of reference for an appeal, from one branch of the family to another and with a view to maintaining their kinship. To maximize the force of that appeal, its original terms (verses 3–8) are deftly remolded in quotation, by assorted means but to a single end. The most decisive (and frequent) variation consists in replacing Abraham's "to my native land [el artsi ve'el moladeti] shalt thou go" by "to my father's house and to my kindred," with the result that the ethno-geographical opposition between Canaanite and non-Canaanite transforms into the sentimental opposition between nonfamily and family. Rebekah's guardians would obviously find it much harder to reject a proposal of marriage addressed to them as kinsmen than as Mesopotamians, let alone non-Canaanites. Recast into such positive terms, moreover, the geography takes on a flattering aspect; and to allay its terrors even further, the (mis)quoter personalizes each of Abraham's spatial references to "there" into "my kindred," so as to substitute a tie of blood for a sense of distance.

This crucial variation launches the attack that others either cover or carry forward. Of the preventive measures, the most salient is of course the omission of all reference to the possibility originally raised by the servant ("Shall I then lead thy son back to the land from which thou camest?") and ruled out by his master. While even a negative mention might put ideas into the family's head, silence dismisses them as unthinkable—hence also the elision of Abraham's own exodus *from* Mesopotamia, in a speech that otherwise leans so heavily on past associations as to play down all unfamiliar factors, including the bridegroom himself. Note how "a wife for my son, for Isaac" contracts into "a wife for my son," so as to minimize the threat of the unknown.

Other variations, however, pile on the pressure. It is with this offensive intent that the contingency originally envisaged as "Perhaps the woman may not be willing to follow me" now reappears as "Perhaps the woman will not follow me." The shift from subjective cause ("not willing") to objective result ("not follow") presumably reflects the servant's confidence in the young woman and certainly covers a wider range of obstacles, with family veto at their head.

And then we find the shift completed and the implication voiced in Abraham's reply. In retelling, it not only fails to glance at any reluctance on the girl's part but throws the responsibility square on her guardians. "If they will not give thee," in disregard for family claims and heavenly guidance, then "thou shalt be clear of my oath."

With this spot of moral blackmail, so final-sounding in form and message alike, the whole audience (this time, the reader included) might expect the address to close. In fact, however, it brings one line of persuasion to a climax only to usher in another:

> (42) And I came today to the spring and said, O Lord, the God of my master Abraham, if thou wilt prosper the journey on which I go, (43) behold, I am standing by the spring of water; the maiden to whom I shall say, Pray give me to drink a little water from thy pitcher, (44) and who will say to me, Drink thou and for thy camels I will draw too — may she be the woman whom God has appointed for my master's son. (45) Before I had finished speaking in my heart, and behold, Rebekah came out with her pitcher upon her shoulder, and she went down to the spring and drew. And I said to her, Pray give me to drink. (46) And she made haste and lowered her pitcher from her shoulder, and said, Drink, and thy camels I shall water too. I drank, and the camels she watered too. (47) And I asked her and said, Whose daughter art thou? And she said, The daughter of Bethuel, the son of Nahor, whom Milcah bore to him. And I put a ring on her nose and the bracelets on her hands. (48) And I bowed my head and worshipped the Lord and blessed the Lord, who has led me by the true way to take my master's brother's daughter for his son.

The speaker has yet another weapon, skillfully reserved for the last. Again, bringing it to bear marks not so much a shift of ground as of focus and emphasis. The opening itself, we recall, introduced three themes — or, in terms of rhetoric, pressure points — with family bond and divine blessing subordinated to the dominant note of material fortune. The second stage then took up and elaborated the argument from kinship, while still keeping God's involvement in active reserve through Abraham's mention of "the angel" appointed to oversee the mission. Now this reserve force takes over, its pressure judged (correctly, it transpires) best qualified to clinch the issue. Success depends on bringing home the impression that God has been in control all along, perceptibly so ever since Abraham took the initiative.

As the reader knows, this happens to be the literal truth. But truth, alas, does not always have the ring of truth. Just as Abraham's original instructions would not sound flattering enough to the audience, so might the original encounter with the young woman seem too coincidental to establish divine stage-managing. If completely unforeseen, the coincidence that the true believer would read as all the more providential is liable to strike the outsider, let alone an interested party, as the operation of chance. Therefore the servant, like many novelists after him, resorts to invention in order to give the truth a more truthlike appearance. Having just edited Abraham's orders in the interests of moral and sentimental pressure, he now turns the revised version to ideological account: God has realized Abraham's wishes in leading his envoy to the family. The surprise of the encounter is diminished, so that its persuasiveness may increase.

Hence this stage also forms yet another landmark in the development of perspectival relations. The reader's alliance with the servant against the family has so far operated along the informational axis of point of view. Equally in the know about all that has passed since the first scene in Canaan, we have been equally alive (and well-disposed) to the liberties he takes with the facts in repeating them to the ignorant decision-makers: the omission of Ishmael, the premature transfer of property, the delayed disclosure of the reason for the embassy, or the variance between the ambassador's statement and the patriarch's commission. Our initial opposition in viewpoint to the servant has modulated all the way into an alignment against a new opposition exposed to dramatic coaxing and irony. At the back of our minds, to be sure, there has lurked from the start the memory that this new party no more shares the allies' faith than their knowledge. But the ideological division gains point so gradually that one hardly notices its relevance as such. In sequence, the family first appears as an obstacle to patriarchal destiny, but not necessarily for theological reasons; then Laban shows his true colors, but his character still lends itself to ethical as distinct from doctrinal judgment; then the servant shortens Abraham's reference to "the Lord, the God of heaven" into "the Lord" *tout court,* as if to broaden the common ground with idolaters, but how much pressure will this change of terms bear? Only with the overall shift of emphasis at the present stage does this divergence come into the open—though for our eyes only—and the opposition perceptibly extends to the ideological axis of perspective as well. Privilege and true belief now go together, as do their opposites, and the drawing of the line all along the perspectival front explains the servant's last wave of attack. He can manipulate the family because they are his informational inferiors; and he must manipulate them because they are his ideological inferiors. According to their lights, the unvarnished truth would not carry enough weight to induce them to part with Rebekah. It therefore needs refashioning ad hominem into a narrative so smooth and well-made as to bespeak divine composition in their own terms. The semiotics of the plot has to be made intelligible to a meaner intelligence.

This secret motive inferred, the new variations in retelling fall into rhetorical pattern. Given the revised instructions, the first problem is to justify the entire well episode. If directed to the family, why didn't the envoy go straight to the family? To forestall this query, he leaves out the sentence "and the daughters of the men of the city came out to draw water" from the quotation of his prayer to God on arrival. With the original range of choice excised, what remains by implication is an appeal for divine guidance in choosing the right kinswoman. It would do him little good to turn to the family without knowing for whose hand to ask; and who except God could do the pinpointing?

Indeed, he proceeds, he had scarcely finished speaking before Rebekah appeared: here he follows events closely enough, but not without recomposition. In divergence from his own viewpoint at the time, he refers to the (then anonymous) girl as "Rebekah," to give an impression of old familiarity with her name and strengthen the sense of her predestination ("It is this Rebekah, here, whom God has appointed!"). For the same reason, he avoids all mention of the temporary doubt and suspense produced by her failure to volunteer service for the camels: despite the triumphant resolution, nothing must complicate the symmetry between his forecast and her performance. If the believer's heavenly plus may look a minus to others, then even scoring is indicated. Nor does the speaker say a word about her good looks, and even her exertions on his behalf assume the telegraphic form "the camels she watered too." This apparent ingratitude no doubt suggests the common bargaining technique of doing less than justice to coveted goods. But it also has a strategic significance, as part of the general depreciation of human in favor of divine agency. The less specified the girl's actions, the more impressive the correspondence between plan and fulfillment; and the less transparent the girl's virtues to the eyes of the beholder, the more visible God's hand.

The well scene loses its original balance, in short, to become less of a character test and more of a manifestation of divine choice. In the interests of the same rhetorical strategy, after all, the servant in his reportorial role cheerfully plays down his own ingenuity in devising the test and his confidence in its results. Reversing the original order, he now puts the inquiry "Whose daughter art thou?" *before* the bestowal of the gifts, as though he would not commit himself as long as there remained the slightest doubt about the alignment of human wishes with divine disposition. And in the ensuing report of his thanksgiving, he appropriately describes the happy coincidence in terms of God's having led him not "to the house of my master's brothers" but "to take my master's brother's daughter for his son."

(49) Now therefore, if you will deal kindly and truly with my master,

tell me; and if not, tell me and I will turn to the right or to the left. (50) And Laban and Bethuel answered and said, The thing issues from the Lord; we cannot speak to thee bad or good. (51) Behold, Rebekah is before thee. Take her and go, and let her be the wife of thy master's son, as the Lord has spoken. (52) When the servant heard their words, he bowed himself to the ground before the Lord.

The course of events becomes so self-explanatory in remodeling that the artificer will not spoil the effect by pointing the moral. Instead, he gathers the human and the divine threads of persuasion into "Now therefore, if you will deal kindly and truly with my master, tell me." Compared with the neutral "If you consent," to which it operationally amounts, the phrasing is so loaded and slanted as to deter noncompliance. On the one hand, the allusion to the recent divine guidance "by the true way" insinuates the meaning "If you will do as God has done" or even the more threatening rhetorical question "Will you go against God?" On the other hand, just as a Fielding's address to "the sagacious reader" punishes dissent with the stigma of witlessness, so is the servant's wording calculated to brand refusal as an offense against morality. Still—and now comes the final pressure—if they do refuse, "I will turn to the right or to the left": I will take my suit elsewhere, to relatives more mindful of God and humanity, kinship and wealth.

Small wonder, then, that Laban and Bethuel declare in response that "the thing issues from the Lord; we cannot speak to thee bad or good." Where God has "spoken" through the design of events, there remains little room for human speech. Nor is it surprising that, though the material and familial considerations must have had some effect, the narrator makes the kinsmen single out the act of providence. Their world picture falls short of the monotheism common to all the Hebrew observers; their morality leaves something to be desired; their knowledge, thanks to the servant's inventiveness, is certainly deficient; and the consent wrung from them, as their subsequent dilatoriness shows, not quite wholehearted even after the event. These manifold discrepancies in viewpoint, whose reconstruction forms much of the business and pleasure of reading, retain their distancing and characterizing force. Yet their imperfect vision also enters into the final movement toward convergence and harmony. Like all the other limited participants—the reader included—the Mesopotamians undergo a process of discovery that brings home to them God's management of the world.

Contributors

HAROLD BLOOM, Sterling Professor of the Humanities at Yale University, is the author of *The Anxiety of Influence, Poetry and Repression,* and many other volumes of literary criticism. His forthcoming study, *Freud: Transference and Authority,* attempts a full-scale reading of all of Freud's major writings. A MacArthur Prize Fellow, he is general editor of five series of literary criticism published by Chelsea House.

ERICH AUERBACH was Sterling Professor of Romance Languages at Yale University, before his death in 1957. His highly acclaimed works of literary criticism include *Mimesis: The Representation of Reality in Western Literature* and *Scenes from the Drama of European Literature.*

KENNETH BURKE is the author of such crucial works of theoretical and practical criticism as *Permanence and Change, Philosophy of Literary Form: Studies in Symbolic Action,* and *A Grammar of Motives.* He has taught at many American universities including Harvard, Princeton, and The University of Chicago.

LEO STRAUSS was Robert Maynard Hutchins Distinguished Service Professor of Political Science at The University of Chicago. He is the author of *Persecution and the Art of Writing, What Is Political Philosophy,* and *The City and Man.*

MARTIN BUBER was among the most influential and prolific modern scholars of Judaism and the Hebrew Bible. His best known books include *Moses, Israel and Palestine,* and *The Prophetic Faith.*

ROBERT ALTER is Professor of Hebrew and Comparative Literature at the University of California, Berkeley. His books include *Defenses of the Imagination* and *Partial Magic: The Novel as a Self-Conscious Genre.*

ROLAND BARTHES was one of the more provocative French structuralists and a founder of the field of semiotics. Among his important critical studies are *Mythologies, S/Z,* and *The Pleasure of the Text.*

James S. Ackerman is Professor of Religious Studies at Indiana University, Bloomington. His books include *On Teaching the Bible as Literature* and *Teaching the Old Testament in English Classes*.

Meir Sternberg is Professor of Comparative Literature at Tel Aviv University. He is the author of *Expositional Modes and Temporal Ordering in Fiction*, and many studies in literary theory and the Bible.

Bibliography

Alter, Robert. *The Art of Biblical Narrative*. New York: Basic Books, 1981.
————. *The Art of Biblical Poetry*. New York: Basic Books, 1985.
————. "Joseph and his Brothers." *Commentary* 75 (1980): 59–89.
Anderson, Bernard. "From Analysis to Synthesis: The Interpretation of Genesis I–II." *Journal of Biblical Literature* 97 (1978): 23–39.
Barton, John. *Reading the Old Testament*. Philadelphia: Westminster Press, 1984.
Burke, Kenneth. *The Rhetoric of Religion: Studies in Logology*. Berkeley: University of California Press, 1970.
Cassuto, Umberto. *A Commentary on the Book of Genesis*. Jerusalem: Magnes Press, 1961.
Chase, Mary Ellen. *Life and Language in the Old Testament*. New York: W. W. Norton and Company, 1955.
Clements, R. E. *Abraham and David: Genesis XV and Its Meaning for Israelite Tradition*. Studies in Biblical Theology, 2d ser., vol. 5. Naperville, Ill.: A. R. Allenson, 1967.
Coats, George W. "Redactional Unity in Genesis 37–50." *Journal of Biblical Literature* 93 (1974): 15–21.
Cohen, Chayim. "Was the P Document Secret?" *Journal of the Ancient Near Eastern Society of Columbia University* 1 (1969): 39–44.
Culley, Robert. *Studies in the Structure of Hebrew Narrative*. Philadelphia: Fortress Press, 1976.
Eissfeldt, Otto. *The Old Testament: An Introduction*. New York: Harper and Row, 1972.
Fishbane, Michael. "Composition and Structure in the Jacob Cycle (Genesis 16:19–35:22)." *Journal of Jewish Studies* 36 (1975): 19–32.
Fox, Everett. *In the Beginning: A New English Rendition of the Book of Genesis*. New York: Schocken Books, 1983.
Frye, Northrop. *The Great Code: The Bible and Literature*. New York: Harcourt Brace Jovanovich, 1982.

Goldin, J. "The Youngest Son or Where Does Genesis 38 Belong?" *Journal of Biblical Literature* 96 (1977): 27–44.

Good, E. M. *Irony in the Old Testament*. Philadelphia: Westminster Press, 1965.

Gottwald, Norman K. *The Hebrew Bible: A Socio-Literary Introduction*. Philadelphia: Fortress Press, 1985.

Gros Louis, Kenneth R. R., ed. *Literary Interpretation of Biblical Narratives*. Nashville: Abingdon, 1982.

————. *Text and Texture: Close Readings of Selected Biblical Texts*. New York: Schocken Books, 1979.

Gunkel, Hermann. *The Legends of Genesis*. New York: Schocken Books, 1964.

Habel, Norman. *Literary Criticism of the Old Testament*. Philadelphia: Fortress Press, 1971.

Jagendorf, Zvi. " 'In the morning behold, it was Leah': Genesis and the Reversal of Sexual Knowledge." *Prooftexts* 4 (1984): 187–92.

Leach, Edmund. *Genesis as Myth and Other Essays*. London: Cape, 1969.

Levenson, J. "Who Inserted the Book of the Torah?" *Harvard Theological Review* 68 (1975): 203–33.

McEvenue, Sean E. *The Narrative Style of the Priestly Writer*. Rome: Biblical Institute Press, 1971.

Polzin, Robert M. *Biblical Structuralism*. Philadelphia: Fortress Press, 1977.

Rosenberg, Joel. "The Garden Story Forward and Backward: The Non-Narrative Dimension of Genesis 2–3." *Prooftexts* 1 (1981): 1–27.

————. "Meanings, Morals and Mysteries: Literary Approaches to Torah." *Response* 9 (1975): 81–94.

Sarna, Nahum M. *Understanding Genesis*. New York: Schocken Books, 1972.

Schneidau, Herbert N. *Sacred Discontent: The Bible and the Western Tradition*. Berkeley: University of California Press, 1976.

Segal, M. H. "The Composition of the Pentateuch." In *Studies in the Bible*. Scripta Hierosolymitana, edited by Chaim Rabin, no. 8. Jerusalem: Magnes Press, 1961.

Sternberg, Meir. *The Poetics of Biblical Narrative*. Bloomington: Indiana University Press, 1985.

Tribble, Phyllis. *God and the Rhetoric of Sexuality*. Philadelphia: Fortress Press, 1978.

————. *Texts of Terror: Literary-Feminist Readings of Biblical Narratives*. Philadelphia: Fortress Press, 1984.

Vawter, Bruce. *On Genesis: A New Reading*. Garden City, N.Y.: Doubleday, 1977.

von Rad, Gerhard. *Genesis*. Philadelphia: Westminster Press, 1966.

Westerman, C. *The Genesis Accounts of Creation*. Philadelphia: Facet Books, 1964.

Woolf, Hans W. "The Kerygma of the Yawist." *Interpretation* 20 (1960): 131–58.

Acknowledgments

"The Sacrifice of Isaac" (originally entitled "Odysseus' Scar") by Erich Auerbach from *Mimesis: The Representation of Reality in Western Literature* by Erich Auerbach, translated by Willard R. Traski. © 1953, © 1981 renewed by Princeton University Press. Reprinted by permission of Princeton University Press.

"The First Three Chapters of Genesis: Principles of Governance Stated Narratively" by Kenneth Burke from *The Rhetoric of Religion: Studies in Logology* by Kenneth Burke, © 1970 by The Regents of the University of California. Reprinted by permission of the University of California Press.

"The Beginning of the Bible and Its Greek Counterparts" by Leo Strauss from *Jerusalem and Athens: Some Preliminary Reflections* (City College Papers, no. 6) by Leo Strauss, © 1967 by The City College of the City University of New York. Reprinted by permission.

"The Tree of Knowledge: Genesis 3" by Martin Buber from *On the Bible: Eighteen Studies by Martin Buber*, edited by Nahum M. Glatzer, © 1968 by Schocken Books Inc. Reprinted by permission.

"Composite Artistry: P and J" (Originally entitled "Composite Artistry") by Robert Alter from *The Art of Biblical Narrative* by Robert Alter, © 1981 by Robert Alter. Reprinted by permission of Basic Books.

"The Struggle with the Angel: Textual Analysis of Genesis 32:22–32" by Roland Barthes from *Image, Music, Text* by Roland Barthes, © 1977 by Roland Barthes, English translation © 1977 by Stephen Heath. Reprinted by permission of Hill and Wang a division of Farrar, Straus and Giroux, Inc.

"Wrestling Sigmund: Three Paradigms for Poetic Originality" by Harold Bloom from *The Breaking of the Vessels* by Harold Bloom, © 1982 by The University of Chicago. Reprinted by permission of The University of Chicago Press.

"Joseph, Judah, and Jacob" by James S. Ackerman from *Literary Interpretations of Biblical Narratives*, edited by Kenneth R. R. Gros Louis with James S. Ackerman, © 1982 by Abingdon Press. Reprinted by permission.

"The Wooing of Rebekah" (originally entitled "Viewpoints and Interpretations") by Meir Sternberg from *The Poetics of Biblical Narrative: Ideological Literature and the Drama of Reading* by Meir Sternberg, © 1985 by Meir Sternberg. Reprinted by permission of the author and Indiana University Press.

Index

Abimelech, 36–38
Abraham, 11–15, 96, 105, 114, 120; election of, 35–37; servant of, 127–33
Abram, 105. *See also* Abraham
Academies of Alexandra, 74
Academies of Ezra, 1, 74
Adam, 33, 34. *See also* Mankind
Agon, 5, 7, 74, 78, 79, 83, 85–86
Akedah, vii. *See also* Abraham; Isaac
Akiba, 1, 6, 8
Alienation, 95, 96
Alter, Robert, 101, 108
Analysis: actantial, 59, 65; indicial, 59; structural, 58–59, 63; textual, 58, 63
Anaxagoras, 41
Anchor Bible, 72
Angel of Death, 79
Aristotle, 41, 60, 94
Athens, 23, 25, 27
Avestic texts, 46

Baal, 103–4
Bacon, Francis, 69
Benjamin, 87, 89
Bethuel, 133
Beyond the Pleasure Principle (Freud), 82
Bible, 26, 39, 44; epistemology of, 127; and Greek counterparts, 23–42; historical-critical study of, 25–26; narration and, 111; perspectival relations system of, 117–18; style of, 125
Blake, William, 74
Blessing, 6, 75, 78; of Jacob's sons, 106–7; of reconciliation, 94–95
Boman, Thorleif, 78
Brueggemann, Walter, 6

Cain, 33

Calvin, John, 5
Canaan, 35, 36, 89, 131
Catastrophe creation, 78, 81, 82–83
Characters, 15, 59, 111–12
Chosen Nation, 35, 37
Classification systems, 17–21
Coleridge, Samuel Taylor, 69
Competition, Greek vs. Hebrew, 24, 75
Covenants, 18, 35, 38
Creation, 18, 26, 27–29; ascending order of, 28–29; evil and, 30–32; of Greek gods, 39–41
Crossing, the, 59–60
Culture, 23–25

David, 5–7
Day Star, 88
Death, 19–20
Death, Angel of, 76
Deborah, 54
Description, 12–15
Deuteronomist, 1
Divine favoritism, 95–96, 104
Divine purpose, 88
Doubling, 92–94; effect on reader of, 100, 104; in Joseph story, 87–88
Dramatic irony, 90–91, 92–93
Dreams as plot devices, 89–90, 93–94, 103
Dryden, John, 81
Du Sens (Greimas), 65

Ego and the Id, The (Freud), 82
Egypt, 105
Election, 26
Elohist, 11, 74
Emerson, Ralph Waldo, 70
Empedocles, 38, 40
Epic, 14–15

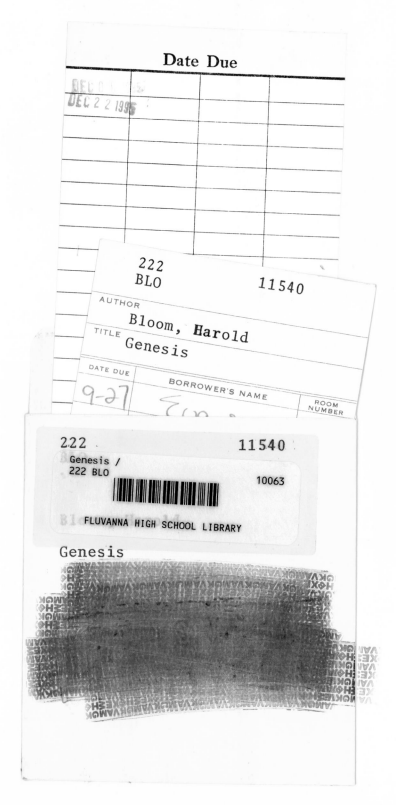